The publisher of this book is generously donating all royalties from the retail sales of **"STRESS-FREE DIVORCE VOLUME 03"** to:

# LEMONADE DAY

America was built on the back of small business. Entrepreneurs take risks believing they can realize their dream if they work hard, take responsibility and act as good stewards of their resources. Today's youth share that optimism, but lack the life skills, mentorship and real-world experience necessary to be successful. In 2007, founder Michael Holthouse had a vision to empower today's youth to become tomorrow's entrepreneurs through helping them start, own and operate their very own business...a lemonade stand.

Lemonade Day is a strategic 14-step process that walks youth from a dream to a business plan, while teaching them the same principles required to start any big company. Inspiring kids to work hard and make a profit, they are also taught to spend some, save some and share some by giving back to their community. Since its launch in 2007 in Houston Texas, Lemonade Day has grown from serving 2,700 kids in one city to 1 million children across North America. With the help of partners like Google for Entrepreneurs, Lemonade Day will continue to spark the spirit of entrepreneurship and empower youth to set goals, work hard, and achieve their dreams.

You can learn more about Lemonade Day by visiting:

www.LemonadeDay.org

# STRESS-FREE DIVORCE
# VOLUME 03

## Conversations With
## Leading Divorce Professionals

By Remarkable Press™

Stress-Free Divorce Volume 03/ Mark Imperial. —1st ed.

Managing Editor/ Stewart Andrew Alexander

ISBN: 978-0998708553

# CONTENTS

# A NOTE TO THE READER

Thank you for buying your copy of "Stress-Free Divorce Volume 03: Conversations With Leading Divorce Professionals." This book was originally created as a series of live interviews, that's why it reads like a series of conversations, rather than a traditional book that talks *at you.*

I wanted you to feel as though the participants and I are talking *with you,* much like a close friend, or relative, and felt that creating the material this way would make it easier for you to grasp the topics and put them to use quickly, rather than wading through hundreds of pages.

So relax, grab a pen and paper, take notes and get ready to learn some fascinating, stress-free divorce insights.

Warmest regards,

Mark Imperial
Author and Radio Personality

# INTRODUCTION

**"Stress-Free Divorce Volume 03: Conversations With Leading Divorce Professionals"** - is a collaborative book series featuring leading Divorce Professionals from across the country.

Remarkable Press™ would like to extend a heartfelt thank you to all participants who took the time to submit their chapter and offer their support in becoming 'get the word out ambassadors' for this project.

100% of the royalties from the retail sales of this book will be donated to Lemonade Day. Should you want to make a direct donation, visit their website at:

www.LemonadeDay.org

# JULIANNE M. MARKIEWICZ, ESQ.

Attorney and Sole Owner of

Markiewicz Law Office, P.A.

**Email:** marklaw@pro-ns.net

**Website:** www.MarkiewiczLaw.com

**LinkedIn:** www.linkedin.com/in/Julianne-Markiewicz

**Facebook:** www.facebook.com/MarkiewiczLaw

**Twitter:** www.twitter.com/MarkiewiczLaw

**Call:** 651/653-4000

Attorney Julianne Markiewicz is widely recognized as one of the leading family law practitioners in St. Paul-Minneapolis, Minnesota.

She is a leading nationwide expert in the areas of matrimonial law, dissolutions involving complex financial issues, custody, spousal maintenance, same-sex marriages, and a specialist in the crafting, negotiation, and drafting of complex prenuptial agreements and all classes of adoptions.

City Pages magazine named Julianne to its "Best of the Twin Cities" list in 2012. She has also been voted Top 10 Best in Client Satisfaction by The American Institute of Family Law Attorneys for two years in a row. Recently featured on award-winning Impact Makers Radio, Julianne advised and led listeners through the pitfalls of the emotional divorce process in an information-packed interview entitled "You're Getting Divorced – Now What?"

Julianne is a champion of strategic thinking and decision-making to maximize recovery for divorce litigants with a close eye on costs. A national leader, practicing law with compassion and integrity, she is known as a fighter and an amazing advocate. Julianne is someone you definitely want to have in your corner in your time of need.

# SO YOU'RE GETTING DIVORCED

By Julianne Markiewicz

*Who do you serve and what types of situations do they find themselves in when they come to you for your help?*

I help married people in trouble at one of the most difficult points in their lives. They are either on the cusp of needing or wanting a divorce, or find themselves facing that decision made by their spouse. In a time of fear and the unknown, I assist people in all walks of life as they move forward in the dissolution process in a strategic, respectful and compassionate way. The divorce process can be overwhelming and daunting. Potential clients come in with questions and uncertainty. Many of them are terrified. My job is to make the process simple and guide my clients through a strategic plan that we execute in tandem. We are a team.

I also assist clients who are walking down the aisle of matrimony and want to preserve their premarital assets or separate assets and define what occurs in the event of a divorce or death down the road.

Post decree matters, or issues that come up following the finalization of a divorce, such as modifying a parenting time schedule, child support or spousal maintenance, also make up a large part of my practice. Clients want new and different agreements memorialized properly in a Stipulation or Court

Order modifying a decree. This is a very important and integral part of my practice.

***What are some of the common obstacles facing the clients you help?***

A prospective client's own fears and anxieties oftentimes get in the way of moving forward -- not understanding the process, not understanding their rights, not sure what to do next, not sure of the next step. This is normal! In my experience, procrastination and what I call the "Ostrich syndrome" are one of the biggest obstacles I come across while assisting clients. "Maybe this will all go away if I agree to go to counseling." "I'll just stay in the marriage until the kids graduate from high school." It never gets better! "If I do nothing about it, or if I don't answer the Summons and Petition for Dissolution, it will go away." Unfortunately, this is not true! "What if I can't make it alone?" You can and you will! "What's going to happen to me?" You are going to emerge as a new and better person! Fear of the unknown is a very powerful trap. Taking the first step and consulting an attorney (most oftentimes free) can alleviate anxiety. Answers are just around the corner. Calling on friends, parents, siblings, neighbors or clergy is also a must. This is a time to rally support for taking the first step. This is not a time to cocoon and hide. See a therapist. Talk to your doctor. Find your attorney!

Another big obstacle that I encounter is the negative effect of anger and wanting to extract revenge on one's spouse. This comes in many forms: dragging out the divorce process to make your husband suffer, fighting for more time with the children to lower child support even if your job prevents you from spending more time with your kids and they will be with a babysitter, wanting to spend exorbitant amounts of fees to fight for an asset because you know it is meaningful to your wife. Really? In the end, bitterness rots away at your own daily life, and ends up eating away at you. Being respectful, swallowing your emotions and pride, seeing a therapist if you need to, and listening to your attorney alleviates a lot of heartbreak and unnecessary strain on the pocketbook.

**How have you been able to help clients through the dissolution of marriage process?**

Procrastination and fear are normal in the dissolution process. Once a client comes through my door, they know that no question is too dumb to ask, and that the process and steps will be explained in an easy to understand format. Once the fear begins to wane, the emotional brain relaxes, and the cognitive process takes over. The puzzle begins to unfold, the pieces fall into place, and the client can relax. It cannot be stressed enough that the timing of a divorce is up to the individual. The longest time a divorce client ever took from consult to the actual filing for divorce was three years. While this may seem to be an extreme example, it illustrates the unique timing of each and every individual. It also highlights the need to consult an attorney so that a potential client is not frozen, stagnant and stuck in the emotional decision making process of "what-ifs" and "I cant's." Once a consult is complete, a potential client may be immediately ready to proceed, may want to think about it and come back in a day, may want to come back in a week, or perhaps schedule a second consult. The operative point is getting in the door. The timing follows on an individual basis. I provide patience and security so that my clients know that the timing is absolutely up to them and them alone. In this way, each client succeeds in moving forward.

The issue of extreme negative emotion and its effect on a dissolution is a persistent and prevailing issue. The ending of a relationship that was supposed to last a lifetime is gut wrenching and disappointing. Wanting to extract suffering on your spouse due to this awful betrayal rears its ugly head often. Here is where we look at heightened emotion, or the "amygdala hijack," vs. reason. As a client, you are swimming in the depths of emotion. As your attorney, I am not. While it may take time, reason prevails. Costs and attorney's fees prevail. Maturity prevails. I once had a case where a couple extracted a week long fight over two dogs and a few marital televisions. Since there were two dogs, the issue appeared to be easily resolvable. However, the couple wanted to gouge one another, and each fought for the dog that they knew the other wanted. Similarly, my client insisted on wanting every television in the house. In the end, the art of reason and the explanation of how much money my client was spending won out. The couple gave each other the proper dog, and I convinced my client that the money that she was spending fighting over the televisions could buy her three new flat screens at Best Buy for a fraction of the price. The lesson? Reason versus emotion. It wins every time! Listen to your attorney.

### *What are some of the misconceptions that your clients believe to be true?*

While counseling clients, I come across many misconceptions. People sometimes conduct research on the internet and believe everything that they read to be true. One such common belief is that "Divorce is easy. We can do it ourselves." It would be great if that were true. If it were, there certainly would be a lot of divorce and family law firms going out of business! That's not happening, is it?

At the time of a divorce, your children and your life's worth are hanging in the balance. Would you trade or cash-in your children and assets for a $1 million chip at a blackjack table, and bet it all in one hand? Of course not! That is exactly what you are doing if you think that the divorce process is so easy that it can be done by anyone, and that it can be done quickly, without forethought and counsel.

Do you really think that lawyers went to law school for three additional years beyond their undergraduate work to twiddle their thumbs and play with yo-yos? Of course not! So why would you think that a divorce can be done easily and swiftly? There we go with the high emotions again. You didn't get married in five minutes, and you aren't going to get divorced in five minutes. There are details to review. I's to be dotted and t's to be crossed. Don't make this mistake. It will affect the rest of your life, and if applicable, the rest of your children's lives.

There are many issues, large and small, that affect how a marital estate is divided: Prenuptial agreements, postnuptial agreements, premarital interests, nonmarital interests, tax considerations, differences in earning history and capacity, what is in the best interests of the children. You need counsel. Don't kid yourself.

Another misguided truth is timing. "We can get this done in a week." Not so much. Remember being in grade school and wanting to know if so-and-so liked you, and placing a note in his or her desk? Remember the way you felt? Heart pounding in your chest, unable to breathe, the ocean in your ears? This is commonly known as the "fight or flight" response that surges through one's body at a time of great stress.

Adrenaline and high emotion, together with the fear and anxiety of the unknown, can lead to erroneous decisions that will negatively affect you for years to come. This is the time to slow down, as much as it feels counterintuitive. This is the time to protect yourself and get wise and sage counsel from someone who has years of experience in matrimonial law. Don't succumb to the fast track urge. It will reach out and bite you later.

Another misconception, and one that has long-term, negative consequences is, "I don't need an attorney." Don't be silly. Of course you do! When your toilet is broken, you call a plumber. When you have a toothache that stretches on for days, you call a dentist. And when you need to end your marriage, you call a divorce attorney. The attorney/client relationship in your divorce is one of the most crucial decisions you will ever make in your life. Why? You need a trained expert! There are many nuances in the law that you cannot possibly be expected to know. The same way it takes a specialist to take your sink apart or an accountant to handle a Section 1031 exchange, you need a specialized divorce attorney to handle your case.

Examples: Did you own your home as a single person prior to your marriage? Did you build a retirement account at your employer years before your marriage? Did you receive an inheritance during the marriage? These are called premarital and nonmarital interests, and are treated differently under the law. Spousal maintenance— do I owe it? Will I receive it? There are these and many, many, many more questions.

Your divorce process can be streamlined if you choose the right attorney. Get on the phone and call some friends. Get referrals. Do the research. Get on the internet. Make the appointments. Once you are in an attorney's office, pay attention to how you feel. Do you feel relaxed (as relaxed as you can be under the situation?)? You should feel welcomed and cherished, not rushed or sidestepped like an afterthought. Are there marble floors and espresso machines? Keep in mind who's paying for them. You should feel free to ask any question. No question is "stupid." Keep shopping until it feels right.

I find that many people choose attorneys that are an awful lot like they are. Feeling comfortable allows you to share your innermost thoughts and fears and share your finances and troubles. In order to bear your soul, it is essential to have and build a trusting relationship. YES, you need an attorney!

***What are some of the unknown pitfalls that the people you work with need to be aware of?***

In all honesty, based on my experience, I could write a whole book on the various types of pitfalls that divorcing couples should be aware of. However, in the interest of saving time, I am going to share three which are likely to be most relevant to your current situation.

First, and I've seen this pitfall all too many times...... You can still trust your spouse.

Ouch. This is a tough one. For years, sometimes decades, your spouse has been your rock, your best friend, your lover, your confidant, your co-parent. You have lived together, through thick and thin, in the best and worst of times, in a foxhole, keeping one another's secrets, protecting one another from the outside world. All at once, that world has crumbled, and unfortunately, you have become adversaries. That is not to say that your divorce cannot be respectful and amiable. As a matter of fact, how your divorce proceeds forward is directly in the hands of you and your spouse. However, at this vulnerable time, you are in separate camps. You need your own counsel. You need your own general and counsel. Nowhere is this more true than now.

A second pitfall that I see often is a couple wanting to mediate their case without attorneys. In the heightened emotional state of a divorce, parties often believe that they can work together with a mediator, reach a settlement, and THEN hire an attorney to draft the final document. This is yet another case of the blind leading the blind, or putting the cart before the horse. Do you get a diploma from Yale before you take the classes? Of course not! While this sounds silly, that is exactly what is happening if you take this route.

Why would you try to hastily settle your life's legacy before you learn the general rules of how a marital estate is divided? More importantly, why would you move forward without knowing how the unique circumstances and issues of your case affect your property division? Once again, the flurry of emotion drives the truck. Never a good idea.

As I stated before, there are so many pitfalls I could share with you today... however, my third and final one is just as important as any other you can learn from... and that is, that saving money is more important than getting the advice you need to divorce properly.

This issue presents itself in a variety of ways: "I'll go online and find a document, fill it out and give it to an attorney to review." "I'll go online and figure it out myself." "I can't afford an attorney, so I'm just going to do this myself." "This isn't that hard. It's just simple math. I'll do a spreadsheet and we will split up the furniture and records ourselves." If you want to build a house, do you all of a sudden start learning how to pound nails and draw up architectural plans? Are you really going to dig a hole yourself and figure out a grading plan?

There are rules, statutes, caselaw that construes statutes, tax regulations, premarital considerations and many time honored principles that govern a myriad of issues on every case. Every case presents a unique set of circumstances that must be evaluated and analyzed for the best outcome – – for you, your children and for the parties. Going in blind like the three blind mice is not recommended. Get educated.

The best thing you can do is to find a way to finance your divorce. Borrow from family. Take a loan against your 401(k) (AFTER you talk to your attorney for the ins and outs!) Attorneys take credit cards, often accept payment plans, and will sometimes work with you to be paid at the time of settlement. This is not the time to cut corners or costs. In the end, it will cost you more.

*Talk about some of the most common fears that prevent your clients from achieving their desired outcomes.*

One fear that I hear over and over again (from almost every client!) is that their spouse is so charming and manipulative that he or she will fool everyone and the client will get cheated out of everything! Whether it's custody, parenting time or a fair split of assets and liabilities, this is a common theme. Oftentimes, with a difficult spouse, disparity of power in a relationship or an abusive relationship, the opposite party is positive that the charismatic overpowering spouse will sway opposing counsel, the mediator, or in the end, the judge. Nowhere could this be further from the truth.

Trust your finders of fact, the experts. Attorneys have been trained to recognize this personality type, and have seen it over and over again. Mediators recognize it almost instantly. Judges know it from the filing of the pleadings and the demeanor of the party. Trust the process and the experts. Your spouse is not infallible.

While there are so many common fears I could mention, this one in particular bears repeating, as I have heard it so often: "I don't know anything about our finances, so I won't get a good settlement." Remember....in almost every marriage, one of the parties handles the finances. It's an age old time honored role. As a result, the other party feels uneducated, vulnerable and afraid. This is normal. This is where you need to trust the process. For every asset and liability, there is a document or an online trail. It is only in the rarest of cases where five billion dollars is buried in the Caymans.

Sometimes watching too much television or exhaustive internet research can cause unnecessary fears. Tax returns, bank statements, credit card statements, retirement account statements and online banking records speak for themselves. In the unlikely event that your case presents difficulties in locating assets or liabilities, or some things just do not add up, a myriad of experts can step up to the plate to assist your attorney. These include computer forensic experts, forensic accountants, litigation experts and economic analysts. A good attorney has a network of all of these experts at his or her fingertips – – at the drop of a dime. No stone will remain unturned. In the unlikely event that a large asset or liability is uncovered after the close of the divorce, there is language that can be placed in your final settlement agreement to protect you from future damages.

A third and final fear, and one that is very real and must be addressed in almost every case, is this: "How do we handle finances and who gets the kids until the divorce is final?" This is a very common fear. Fortunately, a good attorney is prepared for it. Temporary issues arise in almost every dissolution. Who is going to stay in the house? Who is going to care for the kids and when? Who is going to bring the kids to their activities? Who is going to pay the mortgage and the utility bills?

Temporary issues and how they are resolved are very important. It can oftentimes set the stage for the flavor of the divorce process. Are you going to compromise and resolve these issues with your spouse respectfully? Are you going to work on understanding that keeping the family intact, even though the parties are divorcing, is important? Absent special circumstances, the best thing to do in this instance is to keep things status quo. The payment of ongoing liabilities should continue in the same fashion as it always has.

A dissolution often involves one or the other of the parties moving out of the home. This should be done on a very respectful basis.

Announcement of the dissolution should be made jointly with the children. Securing a therapist's advice prior to doing so is always a smart thing to do. This is a major traumatic event in the children's lives. Everything that can be done not to rock the boat should be done. Adult conversations should be held outside of the hearing of the children in all instances.

Negative emotions and anger are for sharing with close friends, family members, the gym and the golf course. Children should never be subjected to their parent's bouts. Oftentimes, in deference to the children, a rotate in/rotate out schedule is put together by the parties, whereby mom is there for a certain number of days, then leaves the house and dad is there for a number of days.

While this is not perfect, it provides the children with an amazing sense of security. Watching for signs of regression in children is important, such as acting out at school, poor grades or a regression in age appropriate behavior. In almost every instance, securing therapy for the minor children cannot be a bad choice.

Strive to be at your best. Rest, eating well and sleep are very important. Regular exercise is a must. Support is paramount. If you are able to move forward respectfully with your ex-spouse, the money issues should be able to resolve themselves on the status quo basis. There are special circumstances, such as when a spouse secures an alternative living arrangement that involves payment of rent or mortgage. In that case, if each party can afford a different living space, they oftentimes move forward as such.

In rare circumstances, when attorneys and parties cannot agree on temporary issues, there is a vehicle available in the Courts for resolving temporary issues called the Temporary Hearing, where a Judge can assist the parties with the securing of a Court Order that governs until the divorce is final. And as we have talked about throughout this chapter, having an excellent attorney that you trust at your side is invaluable.

*It sounds obvious, but why would the clients you work with want to achieve a respectful outcome?*

No one ever said that divorces are easy. Getting a divorce is like buying a ticket to the biggest emotional roller coaster you've ever been on. That having been said, you, and only you, are responsible for the path that you take along the way and the ultimate outcome. Oftentimes in divorces there are issues of infidelity or financial infidelity. These are issues that do not come to light in a no-fault state.

In other words, if a party wants a divorce, a party gets a divorce, irrespective of the reasoning, and a Judge does not want to hear about an affair or the new boyfriend or girlfriend. Gumming up your pleadings with irrelevant facts is a sure way to have the Judge scowl when you enter into the courtroom (if you ever get there). Think carefully before you go down that road. Getting back at your spouse, spouting off angry words and seeking revenge are sure to prolong your dissolution process. They also affect your future relationship and your co-parenting relationship with your children, if applicable.

You may have heard out there somewhere that you are what you think. Nowhere is this more true than in the dissolution process. It is your choice how you control your emotions and how you handle each and every communication with your future ex. Hire an attorney that can set you straight when you need to be set straight. Keep in mind that every communication with your spouse could be a future Court exhibit. Mind your manners. Suck it up. Securing respect is much more important than grinding your spouse down to a pulp. If there are children involved, there is no other choice. Think about it.

### What led you to this field?

I originally began the practice of law in the insurance defense and subrogation field, where I gained courtroom experience practicing in a myriad of areas: arson, products liability, environmental defense and first party insurance claims. I then underwent a divorce personally, and was forced to go to trial for custody of my children. I was crushed that my ex-husband and I were unable to resolve our differences, and learned firsthand the trials, tribulations and angst of a divorce trial. It changed my life. I knew then that I had an opportunity to make a difference in the lives of others. As a result of my own experience, I know what it feels like to sit on your side of the desk. I understand your fears, what keeps you up at night and your worries. My job is to assist you and counsel you from being married to becoming divorced in the most simple, strategic and cost-effective way possible. I strive to accomplish this goal for each and every client that walks through my door. In the end, the satisfaction that I receive from clients that have moved on and flourished-- visits, pans of lasagna, chicken soup, a cup of coffee, Christmas cards and personal notes-- is more than I could ever ask for.

### What would be your best piece of advice to people looking at their options for divorce?

My best piece of advice for someone considering divorce, exploring it or learning that their spouse wants to proceed forward, is to take a deep breath. Take some space. Breathe. Go for a car ride with the radio turned up. Spend some time alone to wrap your head around the decision or the development. Don't panic. Be smart. Follow the steps in this chapter and secure advice and counsel.

For you gals out there, when it is time, round up your posse, confide and cry. For you guys out there, find your trusted friends and meet up personally. If you need a drink, do it at home or in a safe place. Remember that you are not alone! Countless couples before you have gotten divorced and countless couples after you will be divorced. Fear and anxiety are normal. Believe it or not, there is nothing about your case that will prevent you from achieving your desired outcome.

Even your greatest fears and worries can and will be addressed by finding the right lawyer. If, in the middle of your case, you find that your lawyer is no longer a fit, do not be afraid to change lawyers. It is often times the best decision that you could ever make. Your attorney should be supportive, yet firm. Oftentimes, for various reasons, the relationship can break down. Don't be afraid to explore other options if this occurs. A gentle reminder: Most cases settle. Stop thinking about Matlock or Perry Mason.

### If the reader wants to know more, how can they connect with you?

If you or someone close to you feels that they are ready to proceed forward with a dissolution, or is facing the awful news that their spouse wants a divorce, they need immediate support from their friends, their family, and most importantly, the support and understanding of a good attorney. I will lend them my ear and my shoulder, a good cup of coffee or a diet coke and an hour-long free conversation to place them at ease.

The best thing that they can do is to give me a call at 651-653-4000, visit my website at www.markiewiczlaw.com (testimonials from over a dozen clients and a radio interview await them) send me a connection request, read this chapter in this book, find me on LinkedIn by going to LinkedIn.com, or email me personally at marklaw@pro-ns.net.

As this book goes to press, several opportunities to meet with me personally and receive a free signed copy of this book are being scheduled! A Book Release Party is being scheduled for late July at North Oaks Golf Club in North Oaks, Minnesota. Please watch for further details at www.markiewiczlaw.com.

Watch for Julianne's interview in the June 2017 issue of Minneapolis St. Paul magazine, and Julianne's cover story in Attorney at Law Magazine's August 2017 issue!

# JENNIFER MITCHELL

## Family Law Attorney, Mediator and Life Coach - Holistic Divorce Resolution

**Email:** jenny@holisticdivorceresolution.com

**Website:** www.holisticdivorceresolution.com

**LinkedIn:** www.linkedin.com/in/holistic-jenny-mitchell

**Facebook:** www.facebook.com/holisticdivorceresolution

**Twitter:** https://twitter.com/holisticmitchel

**Call:** 708.222.7335

Jennifer Mitchell graduated from University of Wisconsin - Madison in 1999 with a Bachelor of Arts in Philosophy and Political Science. She then traveled for four years, living in different countries and experiencing different cultures and people. Jennifer began her legal studies at DePaul University College of Law in 2003, and graduated in 2006.

After litigating for nine years, Jennifer came to the realization that her role as a Family Law litigator was destroying people and families, and severely harming children.

As such, she utilized her Family Law Mediation Certification, earned a certification as a Life Coach, and applied them both towards her legal practice creation, Holistic Divorce Resolution. Jennifer has formed partnership with a variety of healers to provide her clients with resources to help them balance their Mental, Emotional, Physical, and Spiritual selves during the difficult divorce process. She is committed to helping people, connecting with people, and guiding people to live extraordinary lives.

# HOLISTIC DIVORCE RESOLUTION
## By Jennifer Mitchell

I'm sure you've heard more than your share of divorce horror stories from family members, friends, colleagues, and sometimes from complete strangers. The pain and devastating effects of their experiences leave you feeling the suffering they've endured from a nasty divorce. You find yourself knowing that you also want to get a divorce, but you fear the destructive litigation system. Your fears and concerns are completely understandable and realistic.

Divorce does not need to be a devastating experience for you and your family. It doesn't have to be ridiculously stressful. Nor does it need to emotionally and financially destroy your livelihood and your emotional wellbeing.

Shifting the lens in how you view the divorce can alter the impact it has on your life. Instead of seeing it through the lens of suffering and pain, you can shift the lens to one of gratitude for the marriage. Doing so enables you to be grateful for the personal growth and life lessons learned, and for the gifts received from the marriage.

Consciously shifting your perspective helps you move forward quickly because you accept that you want to live a life authentic to your needs, which may not be the same as your partner. Doing so eliminates unnecessary guilt and shame leaving room for you to thrive when living separately and differently, and understand that there is nothing wrong with doing so with joy.

By choosing the lens of gratitude, you not only set the tone for a stress-free divorce, but you also enable yourself to move beyond your current negative emotional state and transition into a state of acceptance and openness to experience the joys and wonder of a new life. You allow the divorce to serve as a catalyst for change, growth and rebirth. All the important ingredients needed to give you the opportunity to live freely and happily moving forward.

An amicable divorce can be your experience. You can choose not to battle your private life out in front of a judge who knows nothing about you, your children or your family and wields the power to determine the fate of your family. Not to mention the costs as the attorneys are billing you in six-minute increments.

I'm telling you without a doubt that by choosing the right process, you can thrive after divorce. Your spouse can move on. Your children can still feel loved and supported by their parents. You can be open to love, happiness and living an amazing life post-divorce.

Consciously choosing which process you utilize for your divorce is completely within your control. You do not have to choose giving up your power and become another statistic subjected to the abuse of the divorce court system. Not many people know that there is an alternative to the litigation system to get a divorce, one that is empowering and completely confidential.

Holistic Divorce Resolution utilizes a process combining Mediation and Life Coaching, which empowers you, as opposed to breaking you down and causing severe destruction and harm to you and your family's emotional, mental, physical and spiritual well-being.

After having three children, while litigating divorces for nine years, I started to fully understand my role as "mom", and experienced firsthand the importance of my presence, and the presence of my husband, in our own children's lives. It became so clear to me that each parent gives their own special love, joy and guidance to their children, and both parents are needed to raise happy, healthy, well-adjusted children.

At that moment in time, I realized I was contributing to the pain endured through the litigation system. It pained me to think I was destroying people and families and severely harming children. So, I decided to remove myself from being part of a broken system and create one that facilitates healing and nurturing for the whole family unit through the process of divorce.

Motherhood gave me my greatest aha moment to understand parenthood at an intimate level which birthed my idea for my legal practice, Holistic Divorce Resolution. We utilize a proprietary system designed to focus on the well-being of parents and their children to live extraordinary post-divorce lives.

By using Mediation and Life Coaching as the way and means to resolve all disputes that come up in the process of divorce, we enable clients to move on without the lagging guilt and shame so often a consequence of divorce.

There is a common misconception that utilizing Mediation for divorce is somehow inferior or not as effective, or even as legal as being in the court system. Another misconception is that to legally dissolve the bonds of matrimony you need to file a Petition with the Court, serve your spouse via Sheriff, both hire your own cut-throat attorneys to battle-it-out in the Court system, and have a judge decide the outcome of your case.

When the reality is that the Mediation process does exactly what is done in the Court system, and is equally as legal. We attend the one court date to legally dissolve the bonds of matrimony, and we follow the same governing statute. The only differences – which are BIG differences – is that Mediation changes the setting, the process and the tone for the divorce.

Holistic Divorce Resolution meets with our clients in a very comfortable setting, with positive affirmations on the walls, lots of color and nice lighting, water, hot tea, and a library of inspirational books to peruse. We provide our clients with gifts to help them get through the divorce process consisting of a thought provoking divorce journal, essential oils, bath salts, and access to sauna, massage, acupuncture, chiropractic services, and natural remedies. Each tool was thoughtfully created to provide a positive working environment for the couple to effectively move through a difficult process. We also partner with professionals in the surrounding areas, to offer our clients a variety of wellness services to help them get through the process.

We remove the adversarial nature of the divorce that is perpetuated in the courtroom. We help the couple make their own agreements and craft their own Judgment containing the Marital Settlement Agreement and, if applicable, the Parenting Agreement. We inform our clients of the statutory law, which enables them to make agreements that are fair and work for their unique relationship and family. Mediation allows the couple to make the decisions, as opposed to letting a Judge decide on the outcome.

We discuss the statutory guideline for all issues presented in Mediation, to enable our clients to make agreements that are right for them. When you have knowledge of the governing statute, you have the foundation for a productive conversation regarding how the law relates to your unique family. You and your spouse know your family better than anyone else. You have lived together for the duration of the marriage, during the ups, the downs, and everything in-between. Only the two of you know what is fair for you and your family.

Guided by the statute, Holistic Divorce Resolution facilitates the crafting of the necessary legal documents to best reflect your unique situation. We are fully cognizant of our ability to deviate from the statute with the goal of constructing divorce documents that you both feel are fair. Mediation is built on clients leaving the process feeling good, positive and open to new experiences.

Mediation sets the tone of openness and respect, openness to the process and respect for the marriage and each other. We provide the skills and tools necessary to get through the divorce process in an amicable and self-exploratory manner. Mediation can help clients leave behind all the negative feelings and emotions from the divorce by helping them successfully process how the divorce has impacted them mentally, emotionally, physically, and spiritually.

It is important to recognize that divorce is not only a legal process, it is also an emotional process that requires a tremendous amount of self-care and reflection. During a divorce, it is essential to be aware of your four body systems, the Mental, Emotional, Physical, and Spiritual self, and to continually work to maintain balance in all four.

Mediation consists of the Mediator, and the couple, sitting in a room together and discussing every aspect of their divorce. It forces both parties to discuss the "whys" behind their wants. The beauty of Mediation is that together, we achieve results that are individually tailored to be fair and uniquely tailored to the needs of the family.

The court system is unable to achieve such results, because it is focused too heavily on the language found in the statutory law, and is based on the wants of each party. Family

Law litigators discourage their clients from talking to each other during the litigation process, and instead, make all communication go through their respective attorneys. The longer the process goes on, and the less the couple communicates, the more convoluted the issues become.

Couples stuck in the litigation system have their power stripped from them. Once the litigation process begins, the case has status calls every forty-five to sixty days, requiring attorneys to attend the call, costing you more money. Once the endless barrage of pleadings begin to be filed, you will find yourself in a world consisting of extensive discovery, pre-trial conferences, hearings, and possibly a final trial -all with very little involvement from you.

The attorneys are arguing your case, and are drafting extremely hurtful pleadings, containing allegations. Picture your worst parenting day... In litigation that incident is included in a pleading, and is now made part of a permanent public record. Allowing your family, friends, children, neighbors, and nosey coworkers, to read the details about it at any time.

One of the major pitfalls of litigation is that once you start the litigation process, it is very difficult to get out of the court system, and it depends heavily on the attorneys that are involved. Being stuck in the litigation process has negative effects that extend to all facets of people's lives – it affects their work, professional relationships, personal relationships, relationships with their children, family members and friends, and it also affects their health.

The toxic environment found in litigation beats the participants down, and fills them with so many harmful emotions, such as anger, fear, frustration, disappointment, and sometimes hate. The longer people are stuck in the court system, the more these emotions linger and intensify. This emotional stress can ultimately present itself in their physical and emotional health, thus creating illness and dis-ease in the body.

It takes people a significant amount of time to process negative emotions and to move past them. In some instances, it can take years to do so; while others hold onto them for the rest of their lives. Negative emotions deny us of new opportunities to live a life open to love, and deny us the opportunity to live our life's purpose.

In addition to the harm the litigation system causes to the couple, it severely harms children. The court system does its best to help the children of divorce by appointing a Child's Representative or Guardian Ad Litem, which serves as an attorney for the child. However, due to the litigious nature of the courtroom, most often the children are used as pawns in a nasty game mastered by the attorneys, and perpetuated by the court system.

Children are unable to emotionally process the divorce in an effective manner. Divorce deals with issues experienced by adults and understood on an adult level. Children are not able to make sense of these complex adult issues. As such, children will make sense of the divorce with the knowledge and life experience they have up until that point, oftentimes blaming themselves, and feeling very scared, anxious and insecure.

Divorce is extremely difficult on children, especially in the court system. When coupling Mediation and Life Coaching, parents are equipped with the tools and new skills necessary to successfully co-parent in the future. When facilitating the dual process, parents work together as a unified front for their children by focusing on loving and supporting their children and doing everything they can to eliminate any potential harm.

Such a strong focus is placed on successful co-parenting because the reality is that parenting does not end when your child emancipates, as dictated by the governing statute. The hope, post-statutory emancipation, is that your child will attend college, or a trade school or get a job, and maybe get married. If your child has a baby, you and your ex-spouse are going to become grandparents, which means that you are not only going to see each other at all major events for your children, but now will also see each other for all events for your grandchildren.

You have a choice regarding how you want to live the rest of your life. Do you want to experience anger, anxiety and hate every time you see your ex-spouse after the divorce? Or do you want to be happy and supportive for your ex-spouse? Do you want to be open to having a positive relationship with each other post-divorce? These questions are important as they help you to move on. Divorce can mean moving on for both parties. Both can move on to greater happiness, for themselves and their children and grandchildren.

At Holistic Divorce Resolution, we put tremendous focus on the children of the marriage. We help you to learn how to best communicate moving forward, and the importance of being a unified front for your children. We provide you with the skills and tools necessary to best communicate with your children about the divorce. Children need to hear that their parents love them more than anything, and are always going to be there for them. Letting your children know that you both chose to resolve your issues outside of court, and work together to make agreements that are best for the entire family, will paint a more positive picture for them.

Another major benefit to Mediation is that everything discussed in the Mediation setting is confidential, meaning that there will not be a trail of pleadings and transcripts. The hearing transcripts or the like that contain a couple's "dirty laundry" are not in a public record created by the litigation setting. Anything that is discussed in the Mediation room is completely confidential. The only people that know the contents is the couple taking part in the session, it is for no one else to read about and learn.

The vision of Holistic Divorce Resolution is to help people live extraordinary lives, by giving them the skills and tools necessary to seek out their true life's purpose. Divorce is a complete shift in your life. You will not be living the same, and will be living a completely different life. What better of a time to take an inventory of your life? Is there anything else you would like to be doing that you have not done thus far?

Life is short. It is meant to be lived fully. And that includes you and your soon to be ex-spouse. Divorce does not need to be a terrible experience. It is a reality in our day and time.

There is nothing wrong with wanting a divorce to live your life the way you want to live it. You are in control, you make the decisions. Everything that is in your life is there because you allow it to be.

Mediation and Life Coaching combined can effectively resolve issues that often come up in a divorce. Wouldn't you rather gain tools to live the life you desire? Isn't it easier to be happy when you are being respectful and cognizant of the emotions and feelings of your spouse and your children? The process of utilizing both Mediation and Life Coaching has created countless success stories. Couples learned how to live a life of self-exploration to grow and strive to express their unique gifts and life purpose. How about you, are you ready to set a great example for your children? My hope is that you are ready.

As our further commitment to help the process of divorce, Holistic Divorce Resolution Family Practice also creates and facilitates healing events for clients and members of the community reeling from divorce. We offer "Full Moon Burns" which is a powerful experience to cleanse and release the things that are no longer serve us. It's a casual and positive environment that offers people an opportunity to let go of something that they no longer need in their life, or that is bringing them down. It's a powerful step in helping people move forward before – during – and after the divorce process.

We also offer a quarterly "Divorce Open Mic", which is an open on-stage forum, offering people the opportunity to share their stories of divorce. The "Divorce Open Mic" enables people to connect through their stories, experience life by moving on, form connections with others sharing the experience of divorce, and instill a sense of community and self-awareness. Most importantly, knowing that you are not alone and can bear witness to the stories of others, is a helpful way to emotionally process your own divorce.

All information regarding Holistic Divorce Resolution, speaker's sheet, and hosted events can be found on our website: www.holisticdivorceresolution.com. We offer complimentary divorce consultations, flexible business hours, including after "normal" working hours and on weekends. My work also includes speaking engagements to educate people on how to find and make the best choices when it comes to divorce. Holistic Divorce Resolution is committed to helping people, connecting with people, and guiding people to live extraordinary lives.

We are Chicagoland area based with two locations: 1650 E. Main Avenue, in St. Charles; and 1111 Chicago Avenue, Suite 220, in Oak Park. We can be reached via phone: 708.222.7335 or email: jenny@holisticdivorceresolution.com. We look forward to hearing from you, and helping you.

# SUPTI BHATTACHARYA, ESQ.

Divorce and Family Law Attorney,
Hill Wallack, LLP. Attorneys at Law

**Email:** supti@hillwallack.com

**Website:** www.hillwallack.com/supti-bhattacharya

**LinkedIn:** www.linkedin.com/in/supti-bhattacharya-65a5216

**Call:** 609-734-4444

Supti Bhattacharya, Esq., is a divorce and family law attorney with Hill Wallack, LLP, which is a full-service, multi-practice area law firm in Princeton, New Jersey.

She has over 15 years of litigation experience and is an approved mediator for the Superior Court of New Jersey for divorce cases.

She is active in her local and State Bar Associations, and is a frequent lecturer on various topics concerning divorce and family law.

# 5 TIPS FOR A STRESS-FREE DIVORCE

## By Supti Bhattacharya

Recent statistics say that 50% of all marriages end in divorce. That means that 50% of marriages are surviving. What does it mean to survive, versus being fulfilled, in a marriage?

The institution of marriage means something different to each couple. The way a couple chooses to run their marriage, and each person's expectations of the other person, are as unique as the people in it. Throughout a marriage, couples examine their situation to see if it is meeting their expectations. When there are problems that cannot be worked out through compromise, tension and stress can develop, creating unhappiness in each person and often, eventually, discussions about divorce.

Not dealing with the problems which arise in a marriage, through communication and honesty about how each person feels, can reach a boiling point where people begin to act out and engage in behaviors that can lead to divorce, such as excessive drinking or substance abuse, infidelity, excessive shopping, or gambling. Spouses often stop communicating before their marriage reaches this point, so getting through these difficult behaviors is an even greater uphill battle, again creating stress.

There are several keys to managing stress during a divorce. With proper techniques in place, even the most difficult marriage dissolutions can proceed and be resolved quickly with the least amount of psychological, emotional and financial damage possible.

In my more than 15 years of practice, I have counselled hundreds of families through separation and divorce, and have learned numerous techniques to help clients reach the end goal as stress-free as possible, so that they can go on to live happy, thriving lives. The following are the most helpful tips which I have found clients benefit the most from. With techniques in place, you will be well on your way to having a stress-free divorce.

### Tip 1 – Seek Guidance from a Neutral Source

It goes without saying that before you decide to pursue a divorce, or at the very least a separation, you likely will have discussed this possibility with your close friends, confidants such as a religious leader, or family members. For those from conservative and/or immigrant cultures, where divorce is frowned upon, you may have spoken with work colleagues or other individuals who are not part of your personal cultural community, and sought guidance on how to handle the problems of your married life in the more liberal culture of America.

All of these people are important to rely upon as resources, now and as the divorce process progresses, but remember that they all have biases. Any opinion they give almost invariably will favor you and support you when discussing each issue, which is helpful, but may not be what you really need.

Whether just beginning to figure out if you want a divorce or if you already are at the point of being ready to file, I always advise clients that it is important to seek the assistance of a therapist or counselor for a minimum number of sessions so that you can talk about any concerns, apprehensions, or fears that you may have about divorce. A therapist or counselor can discuss and analyze with you the issues which brought you to the point of a divorce, and give you support that is unbiased to the extent that they do not know your spouse and can look at the situation as a third-party. For most people, going through a divorce is one of the most stressful, difficult and painful experiences in their life. The impact which that can have should not be taken lightly, and there are professionals out there to help you.

All too often, people believe that their stress comes from the people in their lives, and do not realize that tension in fact can come, instead, from how they react to those people. Counseling can help identify and analyze these issues so that you do not feel that other people's behaviors control how you feel, thus helping to alleviate stress. Control, or a lack of control, is stressful for many people. Counseling may give you ways to manage your emotions and reactions to your spouse, which naturally leads to more comfort and ability have a clear head so that you can rationally make the major decisions that lie ahead for you and your family.

### Tip 2 – Prioritize Issues

Once you have decided that you need to divorce your spouse, or the very least a separation, make a list of the things that you want to get out of the divorce process, and then numerically prioritize them. If you have children, is custody an issue in major dispute with your spouse, or do you believe that an amicable arrangement can be developed? Is immediate financial stability the most important thing right now, or is retirement a bigger concern? Do you need help to address a have complicated asset structure, such as where a person has invested pre-marital assets into marital assets, or a large inheritance was used to pay buy an asset during the marriage? With a written list, you can break down this process into pieces that are easier to manage. A consultation with an attorney will be easier as well if you can articulate what you goals are for your divorce process.

Without an actual, written list of the issues that are important to you, you create unnecessary stress for yourself because the divorce becomes a massive, overwhelming problem and not one that is seen as individual items that can be broken down and addressed individually, methodically, and rationally. The issues to address of course will be interdependent, and require consideration or negotiation in more than one subject area, perhaps, in order to complete the overall divorce, but without identifying the specific issues that need to be addressed, you will likely have a difficult and stressful time not knowing where to start. Being able to bite off small parts of the larger, and deal with those individually, will help to keep your stress down.

Often times, making a list in and of itself will lower your stress about the divorce because you see on paper that there is an actual roadmap for what has to be done in order to reach the end goal of dissolving the marriage. The other benefit to making this list is that it can be cathartic to write down your thoughts about what you want and why. Talking to friends may not feel the same because they will have input and possibly try to impact your priorities with their opinions. This list is for you, to create and maybe modify as you see fit as things progress during the divorce process. Being honest with yourself as to what you want from a divorce can help deal with guilt and shame that often come from making the decision to end your marriage, helping to relieve stress that can accompany those feelings.

People looking in on a couple's relationship never know what is going on behind closed doors. Spouses are the only ones who know what built the marriage, and what destroyed it. Even in conservative and immigrant families where parents, aunts and uncles, and grandparents may live with a couple or very close by, and may be involved with the daily lives of a couple, it is the spouses who are the ones who lived in the marriage, and their concerns and desires have to be identified and take priority over others' opinions.

I say this to question whether the outside influences in your life should have a louder voice than you when making decision about divorce. If they do, will you feel stress during the divorce process because of the lack of control resulting from that? Are you being honest with yourself and meeting your own needs when you allow others to influence your thoughts and opinions? Divorce is one of the few times in life where individuals need to and must focus on themselves as a priority, rather than managing the concerns of others first.

For people with children, you must take care of what you need from the divorce alongside pursuing what is needed for the children's best interests. Arguably, if you are not okay during and after the divorce, how can you give your children the best care possible? It is similar to how they say in an airplane that if cabin pressure drops and oxygen masks fall from the overhead, put your mask on first and then help anyone needing assistance around you. If you are not ok, you are not going to serve others well. Recognizing this may be another way to relieve some of the stress that comes from negative emotions that can arise during a divorce.

### Tip 3 – Personal Health Plan, Physical and Mental

This brings us to the next tip which is critical to a stress-free divorce. The emotions and pressure that come with a divorce are more than most people have ever experienced previously in their lives. Divorce can be as stressful as experiencing the death of a loved one. Reasonably so, as it is the death of your marriage.

Exercise and healthy eating are important to managing stress in any person's life, but they are of extra importance when going through a divorce because of the unique pressures and emotions that create stress during this time. Any internet search will tell you the benefits of caring for your body as a primary technique to handle stress.

Along with exercise and healthy eating, try to find productive self-care methods to cope, process, and address the emotional aspect of a divorce. No one expects to get divorced when they get married, and many treat the dissolution of their marriage as a personal failure, regardless of what caused the marriage to not work. Cycling in your mind all of the things that went wrong and what you could have done better or changed in order to avoid the divorce, can lead to stress as you are trying to address and possibly undo the past. Moving forward with what you have in hand, and preparing yourself for a brighter future after this dark time, are good ways to avoid the stress that can develop during the divorce process.

Doing something extra for yourself once you decide to get a divorce, such as signing-up for a gym membership or a monthly massage membership, or taking a cooking class, can be a healthy form of self-care. Engaging yourself in things that focus entirely you and your well-being will help to keep stress managed.

### Tip 4 – Hire the Right Professionals

While you are handling the personal and emotional aspects of your divorce, you need professionals to handle the business side. The first professional to consider hiring is a divorce lawyer. While this may seem obvious to some, many people believe that a lawyer being involved in their divorce will make the process more contentious or difficult. The question to ask yourself is what the reason would be to not have help with something you know little or nothing about, and the helper has years of training, experience and knowledge?

Paying a few hundred dollars for a consultation with a lawyer is one of the most important things you can do when preparing for a divorce, as the information gained there will fundamentally guide your decisions going forward. Relying on the advice and opinions of friends or family who have divorced can be misguided and leads to stress because the comparisons may leave you feeling like you got the short end of the stick if your divorce does not look like theirs. Remember, the state you live in and its laws govern your divorce. A divorce in New Jersey will not likely look like one in Pennsylvania, even if the facts seem similar, because the law, rules, and court systems are different. Further, the facts as a litigant interprets or presents them sometimes differ from what actually transpired in a divorce. For example, if a friend was able to retain an entire retirement account in a divorce, that does not necessarily mean that the asset went entirely to their side of the column without having to give something up. It could have been offset against an alimony obligation or another asset.

Learn about and understand through professional advice the elements of a divorce, which can include among other things, custody, child support, alimony, asset distribution and counsel fee claims. With information, you are more in control and not in a guessing game. Rather, you are armed with knowledge and can approach issues in your case without shooting in the dark. Some people want to just get a divorce over with, and believe that hiring a lawyer will only delay things. I cannot say strongly enough how often I have seen high levels of stress specifically generated just because that approach was taken.

A divorce is one of the most important things you will ever go through in your life and it should be done right, the first time, as you do not usually get a second chance to negotiate a better deal or have a do-over trial

Mediation is another method of reaching a divorce agreement, and requires the assistance of a neutral party called a mediator. A mediator is not intended to educate you on the law or tell you what is in your best interest, as they are not an advocate for you or your spouse. A mediator sits with parties, listens to what each side wants, and helps them to reach middle ground, wherever that may be. This is done within the parameters of the law of the state where your divorce will be filed, but the mediator does not represent either party, so it is important to know what your bargaining position is and what it could be, perhaps having completed a consultation with a divorce attorney before going to mediation. Once at mediation, having the enumerated list of issues in hand can be very helpful to ensure that all of your issues and concerns are fully addressed through the mediation.

An important thing to consider when seeking mediation is the power balance in a marriage. Many couples divorce because they realize that they are just not good together as a couple, and are better off living apart, perhaps as friends, even if they have children. These families often can work out an agreement between themselves, or with the assistance of a mediator, and then have separate attorneys review the negotiated deal and recommend any changes that might be needed. A mediator can help the parties to address issues, but if there is a power imbalance, this may not be a helpful forum because the dominant party's personality may be overbearing and control the terms of the agreement. Before any mediated agreement is finalized, it is wise to have attorneys review it to ensure that you are protected and have addressed everything that should be addressed for your present and future. Many mediators are attorneys, but remember that the mediator is not an advocate for either side.

In addition to hiring a lawyer and/or mediator, you may consider hiring a CPA or financial planner as well to help you examine your present and future budget and asset structure. This is particularly important for those with complicated or high level assets, as management and investment will impact your budget. You also can use a CPA or financial planner to understand tax considerations in detail. A good divorce lawyer should be able to discuss a post-divorce financial plan with you, but you may consider reviewing that plan with a financial professional before deciding to accept it.

The next question is how to choose an attorney. This relationship is one of the most personal relationships you will ever have in your life because you are sharing the most intimate parts of your life with this person. Personal references from friends or family who have used a lawyer are always great to have, as that gives you intimate insight into what the attorney-client relationship may be like. However, every person is different, and finding a lawyer with whom you personally feel comfortable is the most important thing.

Write a list of the factors that may be important to you, such as gender, age, ethnic or religious background, educational background or level of experience. Experience with local bar associations may be a consideration as well, as lawyers who socialize professionally with their colleagues and judges can often be useful in helping you to reach an amicable resolution with your spouse. Most cases settle and do not go to trial, so having someone who is experienced in settling cases, and learning about how they achieve that, is something to consider. The stress of a trial is incredible. You must prepare for testimony and speak in open court about the intimate details of your life and take off time from work to attend Court. And then there is high cost involved. Most critically, you give away the right for you and your spouse to control the decisions about your marriage's dissolution, including custody of your most precious asset, your children, by letting the court decide for you.

The right lawyer will help you feel comfort and trust in their skills. They will encourage you throughout the process, and can negotiate a fair and reasonable agreement for you. If you do not feel comfortable telling your lawyer everything, or feel that you must withhold information from him or her, you are creating unnecessary stress in your life by retaining this professional. Call your local or state bar association and do internet searches to research and find the right lawyer. You may also consider looking for social, religious, cultural or community service organizations within your interests, where a member may be a lawyer whom you can get to know in a relaxed setting. Getting to know a lawyer as a person may help you feel the comfort that you need and deserve to help you get through this very and stressful difficult time in your life.

### Tip 5 – Divorce Planning Versus Divorce Preparation

When divorce is on your horizon, you need to prepare for what lies ahead. Divorce preparation is very different than divorce planning, however, and it is critically important to make sure that you know what the difference is. One is absolutely necessary, and the other could create problems and get you in trouble.

Preparing for a divorce involves gathering facts and information, resources, and establishing a support network to ready yourself for the possibly rocky road ahead. In sharp contrast, divorce planning is a legal term of art that involves manipulating anything from finances to custody situations just prior to a divorce in order to create a seemingly favorable or advantageous position for yourself before the actual divorce process formally begins. It is not smart to engage in divorce planning. Rather, it is dangerous and can jeopardize your position before the Court because it typically places a cloud of non-credibility over you.

It might seem reasonable that you would try to place yourself in the best position possible before beginning your divorce, but doing so using manipulation or dishonest conduct will come back to bite you. Here is an example of how divorce preparation differs from divorce planning, and what can unfold when approaching a case under each theory.

Unfortunately, many people do not realize that spouses can change between the time when divorce is discussed and when a filing actually occurs at the courthouse. While there may be discord and arguments during the marriage or during divorce discussions, spouses often do not share just how upset they are about the breakdown of the marriage, and taking steps to move forward with a divorce, such as consulting with an attorney or gathering financial documents, can trigger behavior that is not predicted. Because of this, preparing for the worst case scenario is critically important.

Imagine the following. You trust that your spouse is on the same page as you and realizes that the marriage has broken down to the point that a divorce is needed. While you debate or argue for weeks or months over how the divorce should proceed, your spouse is organizing accounts to try to hide money from you. Perhaps this kind of behavior is completely unexpected because your spouse had threatened previously to file for divorce during arguments, so you thought he or she would be happy if you filed, to get the process moving forward. Instead, once you file for divorce, your spouse becomes enraged and hides all financial documents in the house and changes all online passwords for joint accounts so that you cannot easily construct your financial picture for your attorney. Had you prepared for the divorce well in advance of filing, you would have had copies of what you need, and avoided the stress of this problem.

Reactions such as this are not uncommon. Filing for divorce is the death knell for continued discussions about the possibility of reconciliation, and can feel like the ultimate rejection, especially if the divorce complaint contains specific allegations of wrongdoing during the marriage. People can feel a range of emotions when a divorce is started by their spouse, from embarrassment to anger to disbelief, even when divorce discussions occurred long before the filing. The filing takes away a person's control and belief that reconciliation is possible. The feelings are not necessarily logical, but rather practical in response to being rejected by the person whom you felt would support you and love you for eternity. Understanding the reactions of your spouse can make it easier to address manage your own response, and thereby decrease stress.

Continuing the above scenario, once you have been able to reassemble all of your financial paperwork, which you hopefully can do, you discover, to your surprise, that during the exact time when you were discussing divorce, they removed thousands or more from your joint accounts in the months leading up to the divorce. Perhaps this makes little sense, especially since your spouse reacted so emotionally when the divorce was filed. How could they be so upset if they clearly were planning ahead for the filing? There is no logic to this behavior pattern, but it is predictable.

Clients often consult with me during the phase when they are in divorce discussions with their spouse. To help them manage and avoid the stress that will come if their spouse engages in the behavior described here, I tell them to monitor all financial accounts while divorce discussions are occurring, to ensure that their spouse does not engage in any large transactions without the client's knowledge. Those who are hopeful that the relationship will work out, and are just seeking legal advice to prepare for a possible divorce, often do not believe that their spouse really wants a divorce. Engaging in divorce planning, such as rearranging finances without communicating with you about that, can be a sign that the marriage is no longer viable. Realizing and anticipating this can significantly help to reduce stress during times of marital discord. Monitoring your finances is of course always advisable, but especially so if you are looking at the possibility of divorce.

To be clear, divorce planning is gender-neutral, as are emotional outbursts. Further, no two cases are alike, but remembering that many others likely have experienced a spouse like yours, may help to reduce stress as you are preparing for the process ahead.

Other examples of divorce planning which are not advisable are moving money around to different marital accounts or newly-opened accounts to make funds harder to trace, or giving money to friends or family to "hold" for you temporarily, or paying back "loans" that were given to you by friends or family in the past. If money you received during the marriage reasonably would not have been repaid during the marriage, and you are want it repaid only now that a divorce has been filed, it is difficult to argue that the payments are anything but divorce planning, as they would not have occurred absent a divorce.

In summary, when you are thinking about a divorce, find an attorney who fits your needs and have a consultation. Information is key to preparing properly for a divorce, and spending a few hundred dollars on a consultation is well worth it. It gives peace of mind and quiets the many people in your life, or your Google searches, which give you all types of information, good and bad, correct and, unfortunately, often incorrect. Armed with information and prepared for the process, you can make rational decisions and choices with knowledge and education about what lies ahead for you during the divorce process.

### Next Steps?

If you have legal issues in New Jersey or Pennsylvania, contact me at supti@hillwallack.com or 609-734-4444, and mention this article for a free 45-minute consultation by telephone or in my offices. Take steps now to gather the information you need to prepare yourself for a successful and stress-free divorce.

# KIM M. CIESINSKI, ESQ. PLLC

Founder, ADR Law

Alternative Divorce Resolution

**Email:** Kmc@ADRlawNy.com

**Website:** http://ADRLawny.com

**LinkedIn:** www.linkedin.com/in/kimmciesinski

**Facebook:** www.facebook.com/ADRLawNY

**Call:** 516 308-2922

For over 25 years, Kim has focused exclusively in the area of Divorce and Family Law. She represents clients in a wide-range of matters including, custody, parenting time schedules, spousal maintenance, child support, distribution of assets, pre-nuptial and post-nuptial agreements, as well as post-judgment proceedings.

In furtherance of her passion for offering families in transition an expedient, cost effect and positive option for resolving their issues and restructuring, she now focuses her practice on collaborative divorce, mediation and negotiated settlements as alternatives to litigation for all issues. Having earned a Juris Doctor from Hofstra University School of Law in 1989, she is also certified in mediation from the Ackerman Institute for the Family and trained in Collaborative Interdisciplinary Practice from the New York Association of Collaborative Professionals.

Having a keen interest in social justice, Kim is a graduate and member of the Energeia Partnership at Molloy College which is a regional leadership program. Active in the community, Kim also gives back through fundraising and philanthropy as a board member of Girls Inc., Long Island; the former President of the Huntington Junior Welfare League, Inc. and a volunteer at the Safe Center LI.

# COLLABORATIVE DIVORCE - A POSITIVE PROCESS WHOSE TIME HAS COME

By Kim Ciesinski

So, here you find yourself - the decision to divorce has been made either by you or for you. The future you so painstakingly planned for yourself is being dismantled right before your very eyes. I understand, and not only because I have been a divorce attorney for 27 years but because I have been there myself. You have heard all the horrendous war stories of family, friends and neighbors and fear has firmly taken root in the pit of your stomach. BREATHE... you have options. Not all roads lead to war.

Divorce is one of the most stressful life events, second only to the death of a spouse or a child. There are five stages of grief that were first proposed by Elisabeth Kubler-Ross in her 1969 book On Death and Dying. The five stages are: 1) Denial and isolation; 2) Anger; 3) Bargaining; 4) Depression; 5) Acceptance. Although these stages are universal, each individual goes through them in his/her own order and time. The same grieving process that occurs with death also occurs in divorce.

Unfortunately, the legal system does not have the capacity to wait patiently while people process the grief of divorce in their own time frame. In life, when someone you love dies YOU get to decide when you're ready to shed your last tear and clean out the closet. In divorce, the legal system dictates when the house gets sold and when you must be ready to move on. Shouldn't the decisions that will affect you and your family for the rest of your lives be made by you and your soon to be former spouse?

In some cases divorcing couples are simply incapable of making the decisions themselves and litigation is the only viable option. However, I believe the vast majority of divorcing couples are capable of fashioning their own futures with the assistance of highly trained appropriate professionals. As I see it, divorce is a psychological event with legal implications. Our judicial system treats it as being just the opposite.

The system handles divorce strictly as a legal matter with psychological implications; which, by the way, it is not equipped to address.

This is not an indictment of our system or the dedicated lawyers and judges who work tirelessly to move the cases through the overburdened and underfunded system. Notwithstanding the bad rap that divorce attorneys and judges get from the public and the constant portrayal of corruption seen in every legal television series and in movies, the individuals who devote themselves to this line of work are, for the most part, people who truly care and genuinely want to help others. However, the system just doesn't provide the support and control that the parties need. Collaborative divorce allows the parties to come to an out-of-court settlement aided by legal, financial and mental health professionals who can help them through their issues and move forward in their lives.

### Why Are There So Many Divorce Horror Stories?

When the hammer of justice strikes in the context of divorce litigation, destruction of a family in transition can often be the unnecessary, unintended and undesirable result. Simply put, a courtroom is the wrong environment to address the psychological issue of divorce. To put it another way, if you needed open heart surgery would you have it performed in a veterinarian hospital? Of course not; it's the wrong environment. Although the veterinarian may have many of the requisite skills to do the job, the environment is not equipped to handle all the complex issues that are involved in performing surgery on a human being.

If I had a dime for every time a client has said with exasperation "I am done with this marriage! Why am I not divorced yet," I would be a very wealthy woman who no longer spends her days providing the explanation. The journey to divorce occurs simultaneously on two very different paths. There is the psychological divorce and then there is the legal divorce. Ideally, spouses traverse down both paths to closure simultaneously at a relatively similar pace. In reality, this "ideal" journey is rarely traveled.

Two people on two different emotional wavelengths form a perfect storm for the creation of a divorce horror story. It all starts when one party stalls on the psychological path. The legal system does not afford the space required for the two people involved to reach the end of the journey in their own way and in their own time. The legal system imposes arbitrary deadlines in order to force a conclusion of every case. Even with this stringent focus on progress and conclusion the system is extremely backlogged.

For the person who faces the prospect of divorce stunned and/or hemorrhaging sorrow, the path towards a psychological divorce is long and filled with many emotional land mines. Figuratively speaking, when one of these emotional land mines explodes, it spews shrapnel, inflicting devastating emotional injuries. Such pain and suffering takes a very long time to heal. If you are barely managing to make your way down this road and you are consumed with the business of emotional healing, the legal road to divorce can be nothing short of torturous for you. When someone stalls in a stage of grief or someone races to the end of the legal road and is impatient, the stage is set for stagnation, frustration and anger. It is this particular set of circumstances that lies at the heart of every divorce horror story ever told.

You know the ones I'm talking about – couple married for seven years and takes eight years to get divorced because they fought over the snow blower. How about the couple who spends ten years fighting over a child only to have the war end when the child turns eighteen, essentially aging themselves out of the system and their parent's war? These are classic examples of what happens when people stall along the psychological road to divorce. If you are having difficulty emotionally coping with the end of your marriage, you may unwittingly, if not purposefully, use your emotional turmoil to impede progress down the road that leads to the legal end of your marriage. Inevitably, if your spouse is waiting at the finish line impatiently tapping his/her foot, a Judge is not going to be very tolerant of your timetable.

Conversely, some people often reach a place of emotional closure long before they obtain legal closure in the form of a Judgment of Divorce. These people are D.O.N.E. - DONE! The complexity of the legal procedures that need to occur before they can be declared divorced is of no interest whatsoever to the person who wants to be divorced yesterday. Our legal system is nothing if not excruciatingly slow. The frustration and anger that results from this reality often leads to impulsivity and poor decision making by the person who is desperate to end it.

To those of you who "just want it over," take a deep breath and be mindful of the fact that it took you a long time to get to where you now find yourself. Use this time to reflect on what went wrong and the lessons you hopefully have learned. Try to empathize with the fact that although you may be waiting impatiently at the psychological finish line, your spouse (the person you once loved) may have just stepped on an emotional landmine and is busy digging shrapnel from his/her soul.

### The Devil You Know Is Better Than the Devil You Don't

There are many reasons why people decide to stay in an unhappy marriage – fear, complacency, hope and obligation to name a few. The longer I practice in this area, the more I realize that a fast growing reason is fear of the judicial system and the preconceived notion that every divorce must be or inevitably becomes a bloodbath. Sadly, this view is often true.

Litigation is a polarizing force that does nothing to foster a cooperative future for the couple and their children and gives strangers control over the decisions that determine your future. A growing segment of the unhappily married population is reluctant to subject themselves to lawyers and "the system," so they stay in unhappy and oftentimes unhealthy marriages to avoid becoming a living statistic with the battle scars to prove it.

The legal system, by its very nature, is designed to produce a winner and a loser. In the context of divorce litigation, the winner is defined as the party who walks away with "the most" - most money, most widgets and most time with the children. However, this win/lose paradigm is an untenable fit in divorce, especially where there are children involved. When there is a perceived winner and loser, the entire family suffers emotionally and financially. The perceived loser can often experience anger and resentment which decreases the likelihood of compliance with Court orders, and increases the likelihood of a future filled with ongoing conflict.

You have a new life to build. The last thing you want or need is to carry the anger and the battle into your new life. Every divorcing person envisions a new life that will bring them peace and happiness. Believe it or not the end of your marriage and how you choose to exist in that experience forms the foundation for your new life. Think about it – if your marriage ends in anger and resentment your future will be built upon that same experience.

### Does It Have To Be That Way?

No, it absolutely does not have to be that way. Fortunately, alternative process options such as mediation and Collaborative divorce are taking hold. Mediation is increasingly prevalent, and now, Collaborative practice is achieving heightened interest by providing a more expedient and less expensive alternative to litigation. Collaborative divorce offers significant psychological and financial benefits to divorcing couples and most importantly, their children.

Although you may not be able to even imagine it right now, but after toiling more than two decades in this area of law I can honestly say with a straight face that your divorce can be a healing and positive experience. Oh, don't get me wrong, it's not going to be easy. In fact, it takes herculean strength and maturity, as well as boundless patience and compassion for your, soon to be ex-spouse. However, it is well worth it because the rewards it reaps will be felt the rest of your life.

When a marriage ends, an opportunity presents itself for the restructuring of a family in a positive, thoughtful and constructive manner. Collaborative divorce provides the means to make this happen. However, like many other societal issues, the subjective circumstances of divorce matters exist on a spectrum with outliers residing on either end. On one end, are the cases involving high functioning, emotionally sound individuals capable of reaching mutually beneficial resolutions independent of any formal legal proceedings? It is in these narrow cases that mediation serves as a cost effective, expedient and often highly successful process option.

On the other end of the spectrum, are the highly litigious, often emotionally unstable and psychologically impaired people. These litigants are motivated primarily by hatred and a hunger for vengeance. More often than not, they are incapable of reaching an agreement on even the most rudimentary issues. For these individuals, a trial is the only appropriate resolution of issues.

In the middle, lie the vast majority of cases possessing varying degrees of complexity and psychological functioning of the parties. It is in these cases that Collaborative practice can provide a better resolution and assist in the creation of a successful and healthy bi-nuclear family. The Collaborative process is a relatively young option in family law. This non-litigious option allows divorcing couples to restructure their families and define their future relationship in a positive manner that not only benefits the family, but ultimately, society as a whole.

### How Is Collaborative Divorce Different From Litigation?

Let me start by defining litigation. Many people don't consider themselves to be in litigation if they have never stepped foot in a court house. However, the moment a Summons for Divorce is filed, you have commenced litigation and the system's deadlines and rules take the driver's seat.

Parties in litigation engage in "position based bargaining" which is "I" oriented and focused on the need to win. The attorneys are adversaries fighting to achieve as many of their client's objectives as possible by all legal means available. The parties have no interest in the future well-being of each other. Deconstructing the financial and parental relationship is not a means to an end. Rather, it is the end unto itself.

A great example of the "I must win" attitude occurs in custody cases. In many litigated custody cases, one or both parties will make untrue allegations against the other party in an attempt to gain custody. Although the party making the allegation has the legal burden of proving the truth of the allegation, oftentimes the allegation itself takes on a life of its own and colors the opinions of the professionals involved and unfairly influences the trajectory of the case, even if unproven.

If someone makes a false allegation of child abuse against the other parent, that allegation, although unproven, casts a shadow on how the accused's story gets told. The accused is placed in the impossible position of needing to prove the non-existence of the alleged act. In divorce litigation, the attorneys for each party have a theory of the case and an agenda to advance on behalf of their clients. How they frame their client's position and theory of the case has a direct impact on the attorney for the child and the forensic psychologist, both of whom will formulate their own opinions based upon their personal perspective on the "facts" being presented. If the theory of a custody case is based upon an allegation of abuse, everything that happens in the case lines up behind that allegation. All the players make judgments and form opinions that affect how they tell your story. Ultimately, a Judge is charged with determining the truth through the prism of individual narratives.

The problem with this in the context of custody litigation is that strangers are making their own internal judgments of the facts as presented which then serve as the foundation of their personal opinions. This is a reality of litigation that the public is increasingly rejecting. No one wants strangers to have the power to make the decision of by whom and how their children will be raised. Collaborative divorce practice provides a solution that places those questions into the hands of the parents, which is where it belongs.

Collaborative divorce involves "interest based bargaining," which is "we" oriented – as in, "we need a solution that works for everyone." Differences are treated as sources of potential solutions rather than sources of conflict and opportunity for victory. The aim here is a win-win mutually acceptable resolution. Neither party comes out the winner or the loser. "Interest based bargaining" focuses on the needs of the children and looks to expand the "financial pie" so that individual loss is minimized and mutual gain is maximized.

### What Are The Main Benefits Of Collaborative Divorce?

Collaborative divorce is a voluntary process where the rules of engagement are decided by the parties and not the legal system. Parties engaging in the Collaborative process agree, at the outset, not to litigate by executing a participation agreement. Neither party waives their right to litigate, but should either party do so, the attorneys are disqualified from further representation and the Collaborative process ends. By taking the threat of litigation off the table, the parties' interests are aligned from day one.

Both parties in Collaborative practice are represented by an attorney who serves as an advisor rather than a gladiator. The attorneys are team mates not adversaries. In the context of Collaborative divorce, the parties have identified finding a mutually beneficial solution as their highest priority. Each attorney advises their client about the law, how to prioritize objectives and achieve the best outcome, but it is never done to the detriment of their spouse.

The Collaborative divorce process provides support for the parties to control the resolution of their matter with the assistance of the appropriate professionals in a private setting. Attorneys, mental health and financial professionals work together to help parties going through a divorce gain control over how they restructure their financial and parenting relationship into a new family paradigm. When divorcing couples are empowered to speak for themselves and find solutions that serve the interests of all involved, there simply is no space for the distraction of false accusations.

There are many advantages to Collaborative law. These include the following:

**Cost and length of time to resolution:** On average, the length and cost of a case are about a third of that in litigation. Initially, the retention of the team is a large outlay of funds, but overall the total cost is significantly less than litigation. The well-defined protocols of the Collaborative paradigm allow for an extremely efficient use of time. There is no time wasted waiting around in the courthouse hallway for your case to be called in for a conference where progress is very rarely made. There are no depositions or motion practice.

**Client driven negotiations.** Collaborative practice shifts the focus from attorney driven negotiations to client driven negotiations. With counsel and assistance from attorneys, the parties are placed in control of brainstorming ideas for how to restructure in a completely private setting. Logically, parties who are active participants in the decision making process are far more likely to satisfy their obligations than are those who have had a judicial determination of how to restructure imposed upon them.

**Privacy and self-determination.** Another key benefit of the Collaborative process is the preservation of privacy. Privacy is often paramount in the mind of privately held business owners. In litigated divorce cases involving closely held businesses, a forensic valuation of the business is typically performed by a professional assigned by the Court to act in the capacity of a "neutral" expert. Quite often neither party will be satisfied with the results of the neutral's report and one or both may opt to hire independent experts in the hope of receiving a more favorable result. Not only is the cost of the valuation process and ensuing trial often financially devastating to the parties, but the complete invasion of privacy may lead to the discovery of issues that render the parties vulnerable to legal liability on ancillary issues. In the Collaborative process, all financial discovery provided and information gathered in the valuation of a business remains private, affording business owners the obvious benefit of removing the angst of potential liability concerns.

**Emotional guidance.** Undisputedly, family is the foundation of our society. Although 1 in 2 marriages in the United States end, divorce remains highly stigmatized and viewed as a societal ill, emblematic of the shameful decay of society's foundation, rather than as a normal and predictable life event.

The Collaborative process provides a safe and supportive environment where the feelings and behaviors naturally attendant to the process of divorce are expected, considered a normal part of the process and handled appropriately by professionals specifically trained to do so. With the assistance of a mental health professional acting in the role of a "coach," Collaborative practice allows for the normalization of the parties' emotions and empowers them to move through the stages of grief in a satisfying manner that fosters healing and closure. The services provided by a mental health professional are invaluable when it comes to crafting custodial and parental access schedules. When emotions are given their due, new avenues of communication open up and a positive agreement built on respect and mutual satisfaction can result.

**Financial expertise.** In many divorce matters, the financial picture is complex and the services of a Certified Financial Planner are required. In these instances, the appropriate Collaboratively trained financial expert comes to the table and offers assistance in formulating new budgets and navigating towards financially sound solutions, thereby serving the interests of both parties.

Overall, in the Collaborative process, clients have at their disposal a highly qualified interdisciplinary team to help them think outside of the box and find creative solutions that serve to restructure their family in the least emotionally damaging and most cost efficient manner possible.

"Other things may change us, but we start and end with the family"-Anthony Brandt

### Who Is A Good Candidate For Collaborative Divorce?

- Do you want to divorce with dignity?

- Do you want to divorce in privacy?

- Do you want to plan your own future?

- Do you want to set a positive example of conflict resolution and problem solving for your children?

- Do you want to process your grief and get past your self-limiting anger in a healthy, forward moving manner with the coaching of a mental health professional?

- Do you want to restructure your family and not destroy it?

- Do you want to co-parent with your former spouse in a peaceful manner that affords your children the security they had before the divorce?

- Do you want to plan for the financial security of you and your children with the help of a financial expert?

- Do you want to start a new life whole and healthy?

If you answered yes to any or all of the foregoing questions a Collaborative divorce is absolutely appropriate for your family. If you are determined to have a dignified divorce based on mutual respect, conducted on your timetable in a private process where you actively participate, then litigation is not for you.

### Collaborative Divorce Is Not For Everyone

As beneficial as Collaborative divorce is, it is not for everyone. Experts may differ but in my opinion, Collaborative divorce is inappropriate or likely to fail in situations involving the following:

- Active domestic violence

- Unwillingness to be completely honest and transparent regarding assets and income. The foundation of Collaborative divorce is 100% transparency. If one party is lying or withholding information the process must be terminated.

- Serious psychiatric diagnosis (e.g., bipolar, major depression) which is not medicated or unresponsive to medication.

- Serious personality disorder (e.g., borderline or histrionic personality)

- Active substance abuse

- Either party is fundamentally dishonest or is using the process to delay the divorce

- Either party is prone to blaming and has an inability to accept responsibility for their behavior which contributed to the breakdown of the marriage.

If any of the foregoing circumstances exist, the parties are unwilling or incapable of reaching a resolution that is "good enough" and probably require the win/ lose paradigm of litigation. In my opinion, situations involving domestic violence require the protections of the system.

### How to Find a True Collaborative Attorney

Lawyers are metaphoric gladiators; hired guns by training and in practice. Years of habitual attitudes about the proper role of attorneys and clients and beliefs about what is possible and impossible are deeply ingrained and very difficult to unlearn. Nonetheless, this is exactly what a Collaborative attorney must do.

Although there are many lawyers who call themselves Collaborative after taking the basic training, few have made the necessary commitment to transform themselves and retool their practices. Making the paradigm shift from litigator to collaborator requires a massive commitment to providing a service to clients that is wholeheartedly embraced as a "better way."

Collaborative attorneys who are serious about the process, are availing themselves of ongoing advanced training opportunities and are actively promoting the process and handling collaborative cases. Dedicated collaborative attorneys have affiliated themselves with a practice group comprised of like-minded professionals who are equally as committed to the belief that Collaborative divorce is a better way.

When researching collaborative attorneys, look for those who are actively involved in promoting the process individually and through their firm. You want to be represented by someone who is passionate about the process and the many benefits it bestows upon all those who participate. Interview both collaborative and litigation attorneys and ask what they see as being the differences between the two process options. Their answers will reveal not only their knowledge, but their level of commitment to either process. The guidance you receive and the decisions you make at this junction literally determine how you will lead the rest of your life. Pay close attention to how you connect with each attorney you interview and how you feel when they describe to you how they will achieve your stated objectives.

### Life after Divorce

I know it doesn't seem like it now but there is life after divorce. Someday you will be happy again and may find yourself in a new loving and healthy relationship. Divorce is a fabulous opportunity for reinventing yourself. A clean slate can be very exciting. The sooner you process your grief the sooner you can get on with the work of building your future. The animosity and sense of loss engendered by litigation often delays a person's ability to move forward. Scars from battle inflicted wounds are hard to heal. Your family will begin to heal much faster if the manner in which you ended your marriage and restructured your family was based on respect, honesty and compassion. The knowledge that you and your spouse worked together instead of fighting each other to the bitter end will serve as a solid foundation for your new beginning.

As the lyric goes – "every new beginning comes from some other beginning's end. " – Dan Wilson

To learn more about how you can restructure your family in a positive and private manner, contact Kim for a free one hour consultation at:

ADR Law

Kmc@ADRlawNy.com

516-308-2922

# KATERINA FAGER

Marriage and Family Therapist and Divorce Mediator, Therapy with Katerina Fager

**Email:** Katerinafager@gmail.com

**Website:** www.KaterinaFager.com

**LinkedIn:** Katerina Fager

**Facebook:** Blog Therapy with Katerina Fager

**Call:** 773 952 1450

Katerina Fager is a Marriage and Family Therapist, Divorce Mediator, Blogger and Speaker practicing in Chicago, Illinois. Originally from the Czech Republic, Katerina graduated from Northeastern Illinois University in Chicago with a Master's Degree in Marriage and Family Therapy and completed her Divorce Mediation training at Northwestern University.

Katerina works with individuals, couples and families struggling with relationship issues, or going through a divorce.

She helps clients to develop some new skills and new ways to communicate and grow to create more satisfying relationships, communicate and co-parent well after a divorce. Especially when they have children.

# HOW TO COMMUNICATE AND CO-PARENT WITH YOUR EX-PARTNER AFTER A DIVORCE

By Katerina Fager

I am a Marriage and Family Therapist and also a Divorce Mediator. I specialize in helping individuals or couples who are experiencing challenges and difficulties as they pass through the different stages of life and their relationship. We all pass through different stages in our life and one of those stages is sometimes divorce. I help individuals, couples, and families to develop some new skills or new ways to communicate and grow to create more satisfying relationships. Many of us have gone through experiences that leave us feeling stuck, unmotivated, or without hope for a change.

After many years of being married, couples sometimes feel disconnected, don't communicate well, argue because of every small thing and lack intimacy, or deal with infidelity. If you don't take care of your relationship, it will become rusty and needs some fixing. When you have children they are all of a sudden the center of your universe and your relationship is nowhere near. You are stressed from work and consumed by everyday chores and this leaves you tired, exhausted and in no mood to even have a good conversation with your partner. You have no time for each other as it is hard to find time to even have a date night with your partner. Every small thing can be very irritable and you might find each other arguing all the time. When you argue, you are not intimate and this becomes another reason to feel even more disconnected.

This is the time when Couples Counseling can help and all of those issues can be worked on. It is important to find time for each other and make some arrangements, so you two can have a date night and work on your relationship. It is not easy work, but if you are committed to your marriage, nothing is impossible. I always tell my clients that it always takes two to work things out.

Unfortunately, sometimes it is not possible to reconnect and save a marriage. The damage was done and the years of disconnection are sometimes very hard to fix. After many sessions and no progress, couples might mutually agree to proceed with divorce. Divorce is very emotional for everyone involved in this process. Sometimes one partner wants to stay married and the other wants to divorce. However, you cannot force someone to stay married. For one partner this stage can be more traumatic than for the other and it is important to seek professional help to process your situation and feelings individually. Your life is all of sudden upside down and you cannot imagine what the future will look like. You are scared of being alone and worried about finances and it's definitely not easy. Especially, when you have children. You fear that divorce will harm your children. Just the idea of your children having two homes might seem crazy to you. The stress adds up when you think about probably losing some of your mutual friends and some of your family members. But hold on, not everyone will leave you. The true friends will stay by you no matter what is happening in your life and you will be surprised by their support.

When couples decide to get a divorce they may start divorce therapy. Divorce therapy may help them to better achieve the end of their marriage in a more healthy way, especially when they have children. During the divorce process, parents are often focused on their own feelings and might not pay close attention to their children's emotions. Children may also feel confused as they don't know what is going on, but they can sense the atmosphere at their home. Children may feel pressured to choose the one parent or to which parent to be loyal to. Sometimes children might feel as their parent's divorce is their fault.

Divorce therapy will help you to prepare for handling different situations such as the reactions of your children, your feelings and reaction to the ending of your marriage. It will help you to accept the end of your marriage without feeling like you have to blame yourself or your ex. You will learn necessary tools and skills on how to deal with your loss. It will help you to eventually see the light at the end of the tunnel. Your therapist will lead the sessions, so you can feel that you are ending your marriage with dignity and respect.

They are many misconceptions surrounding divorce. However, the most common misconception is that you should stay together for the sake of your children, or that you cannot have good communication with your ex after a divorce. It's very hard to make the right decision whether to stay together, or to divorce when you have children. You don't want to break up your family. You are worried what other people will think. You are worried about your children and how they would react to divorce. But, if you are in a toxic relationship and you constantly fight and argue with your spouse, staying in this type of situation and relationship can be very damaging to your kids. Your relationship with your partner is the first relationship role model to your children. If you fight and argue with each other, your children might think that this is normal and ok. When they grow up they might repeat the same behavior, interactions and communication in their future relationships. If you are disconnected and barely interact with your spouse, your children might think this is what a relationship should look like. Whatever you do and how you behave might become the norm to your children. Sometimes, kids feel relieved if the parents get divorced as they could not stand the constant arguments and fights anymore. Whatever you will decide, think about your children.

The other misconception is that after a divorce you cannot have good communication with your ex and co-parent. That goes down to the stigma attached with divorce. We all hope that we are getting married only once. So, when divorce comes, we often see it as something painful, shameful and sad. We see it as a fight for custody and not as a transition to a different stage of our life.

During the divorce process you feel angry and emotional. You want to fight for your children and you want to hurt your ex. But this custody battle only hurts you and your children. Take a deep breath and think for a second how your children feel. Yes, you are very hurt and scared. At this point, you probably don't want to see your ex ever again and even thinking of talking to your ex makes you nauseous. But remember, you have children and you will have to still co-parent with your ex. That means having some kind of communication together. One day you will both be grandparents to your grandchildren and maybe occasionally see your ex. So, with the help of a trained therapist you can learn how to communicate and co-parent effectively even after your divorce.

In therapy both of you need to clarify boundaries and rules with each other and your children. I always tell my clients, even if you don't like each other and have different opinions and views, you still have to collaborate together and forget about the past for the sake of your children. It is also important to remember that at this point, you cannot change your ex-partner and their behavior. You can only control yours. Try to treat your ex with respect and more likely you will get respect back.

Keep your communication with your ex focused on issues related strictly to your children. Don't go back and forth and start the blame game. It's over and it's done. You can't change anything. The only thing you can do is to establish a good communication with your ex. With good communication, there will be less chances of misunderstandings and conflicts between you and your ex. Good communication also means that your children will have a better chance of a healthy and happy upbringing. If you cannot talk to your ex, try to communicate via text, or an email. Try to keep consistency and a schedule for your children and be open in letting your children talk to your ex whenever they want to. Try to be supportive and encouraging to your children to have a good relationship with your ex. Reassure your children that both of you will always love them and be there for them no matter what.

I worked with clients who came with the intention to work on their marriage. They felt really disconnected and were trying to find the spark, or the connection. Unfortunately, after many sessions and no progress they decided to proceed with divorce. They had children and their main concern and worry was how and who is going to tell their children about the divorce. They have no idea who should tell the kids or what to tell them. After long talks they made the decision to bring their children for a few sessions and during those sessions, both parents took the responsibility of telling them about the separation.

Some sessions were focused on processing their children's feelings and the parents answered all of the questions their children had. Children have many questions such as where they will live, where they will sleep, with whom they will live, will they go to the same school, or what is divorce and why are you getting divorced? In other sessions without the children, co-parents addressed the transition for the whole family and talked about the rules and in general about their co-parenting roles. Now, this is the ideal situation and I understand that this does not happen all the time, but it is also something not impossible. I had clients and they could not even sit in one room together. They could not talk to each other or look at each other. They felt very angry, hurt and betrayed. After a few sessions of talking to them individually and validating their feelings and explaining to them that yes, divorce is very painful and emotional for everyone, they felt a little bit better.

I talked to them both about their children and what they are probably experiencing. I explained to them that it takes a lot of effort from both to forget about the past and focus on their children and their future. Communication got much better between them. It's all about the awareness and the effort to do better, be better parents and have better communication for their children.

The biggest fear I see with my clients is who and what to tell children when divorce comes. It is important for both of you to tell them about the divorce. Think about the right timing of telling them and when it is actually realistic. Keep it very simple and stay away from details, kids don't need to know that your ex cheated on you, or that you don't love each other anymore. Make sure that all of your divorce papers are far from your kids' sight, especially when they know how to read. Explain to your children what a divorce is as they have no idea, they have maybe only heard the word. Reassure your children that it is not their fault and that you both love them.

When you are getting a divorce, there are some pitfalls I would like to share with you for you to be more aware of in order to try and avoid them. When you are a parent and you are going through a divorce, you should be aware that your children can hear you, can see you and your body language and can feel when you are sad, upset or angry. You should avoid talking in a bad manner about your ex-partner. You should always keep in mind that bad mouthing your ex in front of your children is very damaging to them. So many parents do that and need this as a constant reminder.

Even talking to a friend on the phone and having kids in the other room. You think your kids are busy playing videogames, or watching television, but kids are smart and pay attention to everything. They are smart little people and they can sense anything especially, if you are going through the divorce process. Children love both parents and it is very hard for them even to process the divorce, or to pick and choose. Some children feel guilty and feel responsible for their parents' divorce. So, talking bad about their mom or dad makes it very hard on them.

You should seek professional help to address your own issues if you are having a hard time. Continued fighting or resentment between you and your ex creates a negative, unhealthy environment for your children and you certainly don't want to do that. Don't use your children as a messenger, or don't put your kids in the middle. Children should stay away from any heated arguments you have with your ex. Do your own communication with your ex. As I mentioned early on, you should always keep in mind that you are your children's first role models not only for a relationship, but also for communication and social skills.

If you are going through a divorce and you feel you can't handle it on your own, you feel depressed, sad, and angry or betrayed, please seek professional help. Divorce is very painful and leaves people drained and exhausted. It is important to recognize it and try to do something to change that. It is always beneficial either to vent to your therapist, or to process your painful experience. Venting to your friend, or a family member is good from time to a time, but be aware that your friend loves you and sometimes can be biased. If you can't go for therapy with your ex-partner and work on establishing a better communication after a divorce, come with your children, because they need it the most. Or talk to your children on a daily basis about their feelings and what's going on in their minds.

During this painful process children might start acting out, or become very emotional and misbehave. Try to be very patient and supportive. As much as it is difficult for you, it is very difficult for them too. They need to process their feelings and it is helpful to see a professional who can do that with your children. Children will talk to you, but might open up more about their struggles to an individual therapist. They might feel hesitant telling you everything as they will not want to hurt your feelings. Spending more quality time with your children during this difficult time is also important. Put away your phone, pay attention and listen to them. Your children might feel lonely and miss the other parent. It is a big transition and adjustment for the whole family. It takes time and effort from everyone involved. But remember, things will get better over time. Don't lose hope, stay positive and better days are coming your way.

If you want to know more about how to communicate and co-parent with your ex-partner after a divorce, then send an email to katerinafager@gmail.com, book a 10 minutes free consultation, or visit www.KaterinaFager.com, or check my Facebook blog @therapywithkaterinafager.

# LORENA R. CARDAMA

Attorney at Law, The Cardama Law Firm
and Legal Edge Coaching

**Email:** cardama@cardamalaw.com

**Website:** http://wwww.CardamaLaw.com

**LinkedIn:** www.linkedin.com/in/lorenacardama

**Facebook:** www.facebook.com/cardama.law

**Call:** 407-704-8932

Ms. Lorena Cardama is the founder of the Cardama Law Firm, P.A. where she has dedicated 10 years of her career helping families through their most sensitive moments which include: divorce, paternity cases, child support and adoption.

Ms. Cardama has taken her experience in creating a successful law practice, as well as her experience in helping other companies and professionals take their business to the next level, and has created Legal Edge Coaching.

She is highly involved with the community; she has been a volunteer of Teen Court since 1998 and is now serving as Teen Court Judge. Ms. Cardama has received awards from the Supreme Court of Florida, the Young Lawyers Division of The Florida Bar and the Florida Pro Bono Coordinators Association's lapel pin in recognition three years in a row, for her exceptional pro bono services, as well as the prestigious Guardian of Justice Award from Community Legal Services of Mid Florida for her devotion in protecting children's rights, 2 years in a row.

She was awarded the Osceola County Teen Court Pro Bono Award from the Community Legal Services of Mid Florida. Mrs. Cardama has been awarded Adult Volunteer of the Year from Teen Court, 2014 Family Law Attorney of the year, 2017 Woman in Law award.

# SENTIMENTS OF DIVORCE
## By Lorena Cardama

A divorce or separation is hard to deal with. We must deal with the realization that life will no longer be the same. We are left to deal with the roller coaster of emotions that come with the divorce. These emotions will impact each person in different ways, in different order, and on different levels. How long we deal with each emotion depends on what part we played in the divorce or how we internalize the "story" that we keep telling ourselves.

I have found in my years of practice that while each person is dealing with their emotions, they lose sight of the end result, which is the pain and hurt that they cause on their children. It is important to be cognizant of what we are feeling and why we are feeling it.

Being able to understand our emotions while this is happening will help us get a grip on our thoughts and regain control of our emotions minimizing the impact on our children. If we recognize what we are feeling in the moment, and we change our physiology, focus on our language, we can control "our story" and safeguard our children in the process.

The following are the 3 groups of emotions that people deal with during the divorce process that can tremendously impact the children.

### *Guilt and Shame:*

Guilt that we caused the end of your marriage, guilt that we did not do enough to save our marriage. You may be telling yourself, that you were not the perfect mother or perfect father. Maybe you even feel that you were the reason why your marriage ended, these are all debilitating stories we tell ourselves.

Shame because you are now a statistic, you feel you "failed" the social stereotype of the "perfect" family. Shame, because you realize that your children will now have to live in two separate homes because of something you did. What I have seen happen is that those with absolute guilt and shame are those who take responsibility for the end of the marriage, those who acknowledge their wrongs are those who give in, those who do not fight for their children because they do not want to keep hurting their spouse, so they just fold. Then there are those that are mad as hell at the person who wronged them and they will do anything to make them "pay" and the best way to do that is to limit the contact with their children, which may cause them even more shame.

I represented a man, who cheated and got caught. He felt such shame for his actions that when consulting me, you could see the tears in his eyes and the shame on his face. I went on to tell him his rights and discussed timesharing. He told me that he would accept anything that she wanted to give him, that he realized that she was hurt and mad and that every other weekend with his children would be fine. He went on by stating that he already broke up the family, that he did not want to cause any more hurt to his wife or children. Of course, his wife was hurt and mad, she was not willing to offer any more than every other weekend timesharing with the children and my client took it. Now, when I asked his wife why just every other weekend, her answer was one of a scorned woman, "because, that is all I want him to have". She was not able to tell me that my client was a horrible father, that he mistreated the children, or did not provide for them..... simply that that's all she wanted him to have.

My client was blinded by his emotions of shame and guilt to see what would be in his children's best interest. He thought it would be better to "give up the fight" in efforts to avoid additional heartache to his wife. His wife knew that she could take advantage of my client's feelings for her benefit, so she did, and at that moment all she wanted to do was to keep his children away. Neither one thought about the children and how it would affect them seeing their father every other weekend, (4 days a month).

Ideally, the mother should have seen through her anger of being betrayed and lied to, and saw him for who he was to his children, a loving and carrying father. She was never once able to tell me that he was a horrible father, so knowing that, why only every other weekend? How was this decision in her children's best interest? Let's talk about my client... the father.... I understand that he made a mistake as a man, and maybe as a father by putting his need of attention/ significance over his family, which caused him to cheat. But how is giving up and accepting every other weekend any different than cheating? He once again, but his needs above the needs of his children. He knew he was a good father, he knew his children loved him very much, yet he allowed his emotions to get the best of him.

The following case, I am going to share with you, is one that I will never forget. I handled this case early in my career, I must have been practicing law for a year and although I always focused on family law, I still had not seen all the ugly that comes with this field. But this case, showed me my fair share of "ugliness"

I represented the wife in this case, the parties had two children who were born during the marriage. My client did not see the divorce coming, apparently, the husband had been cheating and had a new girlfriend. During mediation, we discussed what the timesharing schedule would be for the children, and the husband's attorney throw a wrench in the mix. He requested a DNA test for one of the children, as you can imagine, my client was floored. It was her position that she had never cheated and that he knew damn well that the children were his. I questioned the attorney, where did this new allegation come from? He said that his client did not want to have timesharing with the children, EVER!

My client immediately starting crying, she could not understand how this man she loved, who had children with her in a marriage, who helped raise this beautiful little girls, could sit there, with a schmuck look on his face and state that he never wanted to see his kids again. I almost jumped over the mediation table. I could not believe what I heard. I can't even remember all the things that came out of my mouth in that moment. All I know is that I must have called him a few good names. (or bad names that is). After regaining my composure, I asked him, why??.... Why after all these years would you just give up on your daughters?? His reply was so distasteful... "Because I have a new life now and I do not want to deal with her (wife's) bullshit, I rather give up my rights as a father". You have a new life now, what the hell does that mean?? A divorce from your wife does not mean you get to divorce your kids, your obligations, it's not a clean slate.

Where was the children's best interest here? Nowhere!! It is my belief that this father was so guilty or ashamed of his actions that he ran away as a coward. He had 2 daughters, I can only assume that he could not face them, he could not confront his actions to his daughters, could not introduce them to this new woman, so he ran. At the end he signed a legal document stating that he would not have contact with the children. Unfortunately, I lost contact with my client. I pray that her daughters turned out well and that their father's decision did not cause irreparable harm to them. But realistically, it did. 2 young woman, in their peak of teenage years, the time that they need their father, the time that they need to be accepted and loved by a man, yet were abandoned by him, could only cause low self-esteem and feelings of abandonment.

### Fear and Anxiety:

The unknown can cause tremendous fear and anxiety. How are you going to pay the bills? Which days are the children going to be with you or with your ex? Will the children adjust? How will this affect them? Am I ever going to be able to find love again? What if my children want to spend more time with my ex than with me? There are so many unanswered questions, all of which can drive anyone crazy, if you allow them to consume your thoughts.

Fear comes in all shapes and sizes, and of course, the fear and anxiety that comes from losing control. The fear that your ex will get everything they want. The constant threats that they will take your children away, the bullying and control tactics, the accusations of parental alienation. Some people will go to unthinkable limits to retain control and in the process disregard how it will later impact their children. Your children can tell when you are in fear, when you are suffering, or when you are stressed and as a result, they internalize the same feelings.

I represented the father J.C., he has three beautiful daughters. At the time that I started on the case, his daughters were 8, 6 and 4. The mother filed for divorce and my client was asking the court for equal timesharing with the children. When the mother felt fear that she was going to lose control of her children and was no longer able to dictate when the father could or could not see the children, she created an allegation that my client was sexually abusing the oldest child. The Department of Children and Family got involved and my client was unable to have contact with the oldest child and only supervised contact with the two youngest children. My client was ordered to take a psychosexual evaluation, anger management classes and had to follow a case plan. The dependency court, felt that they had to error in the side of causation, even though my client maintained his innocence, he did what was ordered of him.

After the evaluation was returned, the child was interviewed and the investigation was concluded, it was determined that the mother had made up all of the allegations and attempted to coach the child into testifying that her father had touched her. The Court determined that the children were in danger with the mother, as she was capable of brain-washing the minor child that she was sexually abused and the Court entered an Order for my client to take custody of all three minor children. The day of the hearing, the mother failed to appear, the Courts sent a social worker to the mother's house and it was discovered that the mother had vanished with the minor children. Their whereabouts were unknown and the children were placed on the missing children's list. The FBI got involved in their attempts to locate her. Eventually her car was found, but not her or the children. The FBI believed that she was either in the

United States or Puerto Rico, as she did not have the children's passports.

My client hired a private investigator and eventually located the mother in Guatemala. It had been 4 years since she disappeared. Although, my representation of my client concluded back in 2011, I still keep in touch with him and follow the progress. I was advised that there is a pending case in Guatemala, where they have charged the mother with kidnapping, but as of 2017, my client still does not have custody of his daughters.

Fear of losing control drove this mother to vanish with her daughters. The damage that these little girls will be dealing with will take years to overcome, if ever. The idea that their mother changed their identity, changed their names, moved them from one country to another, and allowed them to believe that their father was abusing them, is horrific.

In a different case, I represented a father, who we will reference as A.N. The mother did not want the father to have anything to do with the child. She did everything possible to keep the father away. My client whet years without contact from his child. A.N. maintained his child support obligation up-to-date and made every attempt he could to contact the child, sending gifts for Christmas and his birthday, however the mother would return the gifts and would not pick up the call when the father was calling. My client also became fearful and anxious about his constant denials. We went to court and the court granted the opportunity to re-connect with this son, as well, as telephone contact. However, the mother continued to build barriers, making it more and more difficult for him to see his child. Our only other avenue was to continue filing motions for contempt and continue to bring her back to court.

A.N. was concerned because even if we continue to win, her behavior was not changing. He did not have the financial means to continue to bring her to court every time she denied him access to his son. My client suggested that he give up his rights to his son and allow the mother's new husband to adopt the child. The mother jumped at the chance and my client signed consent for step-parent adoption. This decision was not made easily. He felt that no matter what he did or how many orders allowing him to see his son, that the mother would not change her ways and the fight would never end.

His actions to give up his rights to his son were driven by the fear that the fight and the constant litigation would never end. The fear of uncertainty, sometimes is greater than the illusion of success. There was a chance that if the mother would continue her behavior, he would gain custody of the child, but the fear was greater and at the end drove him to give up his rights.

### Anger and Revenge:

You have to face it, your marriage or relationship is now over.....you're angry! You're angry that your spouse betrayed you or disrespected you. You're angry that you invested so much time and effort into a relationship that has not worked out. You're angry because your spouse is now telling you that you're not going to get anything out of the marriage or that you're never going to see your children again.

Maybe you don't even understand the feeling you are actually feeling so you're just mad! Sometimes people need to feel angry to justify their desire to leave the relationship... "I just can't stand him anymore, he makes me so mad!"

Often times I have witnessed where one person does not want to let go of the connection they have with their ex. Because the line between love and hate is so thin and both are such strong emotions, they allow that love and obsession to convert into hate and revenge and thus keeping their connection.

Keeping an emotional connection to their partner, whether negative or not, is better than not having a connection at all. Let's think about it for a minute...when you are fighting with someone, you continuously send text messages or emails, you find things to say that you know will push the right buttons with your partner, that will cause a reaction. That reaction causes them to text or email back because they want to prove their point, or call you whatever name they are thinking in that moment. Once the response goes out, you will likely respond back and the cycle will continue until one of you has had enough of that conversation. Then, 1 or 2 days later a new subject will arise that will cause restart the cycle. All and all, the constant back and forth of accusations will allow for the connection to stay alive. As long as the connection never dies, you still have a piece of them which fosters a very toxic situation.

I am going to share two cases in which I strongly believe that the mothers were not able to let go of the connection that they have to the father's. By not letting go, the have involved their child(ren) and cause years of unnecessary litigation.

The following is the story of J.M. The mother decided that she did not want the father to be a part of their daughter's life. She stated that JM was smoking weed and that it was not in the best interest of the child to be around him. What she forgot to mention is that she also smoked weed when they were together. Because JM was not able to provide the court with a clean drug test, he was forced to see his daughter by supervised visitation at the supervising center, which meant that the minor child would visit her dad 2 hours every Saturday, in a school that requires the minor child to pass through metal detectors. They are confined to a fenced park, surrounded by parents who use cocaine and meth and parents who have abused their children. Prior to the supervised visitation, it had been 6 months since my client had seen his daughter.

In hearing all the facts, as a parent, we need to ask ourselves, who is this really benefiting? The mother stated that she was concerned about the best interest of the child. Do you really think that it is in your child's best interest to go half a year without seeing her father and then when she finally gets the opportunity, the visitation is not in a place where she can be comfortable and able to run free, instead she is surrounded by drug users and abused children?

This is an obvious case of a woman scorned. If you did not have a problem with the father when you smoked weed with him, why are you concerned now? There was a time in the 2 ½ year litigation that, the mother wanted to relocate to a different State. In order for her to do so, she would need permission from my client or from the court. In efforts to get an agreement from my client, she offered unsupervised timesharing with the child. J.M. was to get the remainder of the summer, spring break, half of the winter break, and 3 weeks in the summer of the following year and thereafter. She stated that JM could visit their child in the new State at any time with prior notice. So let me see if I get this straight, he's unfit to care for your child because he smokes weed while you live in the same State, but he is ok to care for the child unsupervised because you want to chance tail and move to another State?.... how does this even make sense?

The mother relocated to a different State for a period of time, but refused to sign the parenting plan, causing the litigation to continue for another year. If you moved already, why keep fighting? Why stay married? Well, she moved back and as you can imagine made it even more difficult for my client to see his child. The case finally reached the end stage... trial! However, we were able to reach an agreement prior to the trial commencing. It took a lot of work between me and the other attorney, but we reached what we believed was a fair resolution to the case. My client would see the minor child supervised by the mother for 4 weekends and then unsupervised and eventually overnights, when he produced a clean drug test.

Let's remember, that the mother thought that my client was completely incapable of caring for the needs of a 6-year-old because he occasionally smoked weed on days that he did not have the child... you know, because weed has a lingering affect for days and days.... NOT! Anyways, you would think or at least hope that this would bring a resolution to the case, closure and peace for them to move on.... But NO... she has found other ways to get under my client's skin, such as... blocking him from her cell phone so he could not contact the child, dictating where the timesharing would take place... hovering over the child when the father is spending time with her... I can go on and on.

Her behavior is absolutely ridiculous, how is this helping the child? She was not concerned about her ability to care for the needs of the child when she would smoke weed or when her current boyfriend smokes weed. This mother has gone so far as to contact J.M.'s new girlfriend to accuse him of cheating on her... really??!! Why? Even if he did cheat, what is it to you? Why spend so much energy on a person? Well, the answer is clear, she is doing everything possible to continue to have a connection with him. The more she makes his life impossible the longer they will stay connected.

Personally, I find it extremely sad, that after a year of litigation and having a new relationship, she is not able to let go of her feelings to live a happy and peaceful life.

This mother could have done so many things differently. Starting by letting go of the hatred and allowing the father to spend time with the child. She never brought forth allegations that the father was mistreating the child, or neglectful, just that he smoked weed. All he wanted was to have time with the child every week. He wasn't even pushing for a 50/50 split, just a consistent schedule, where he would be a permanent and stable father in his child's life.

Now, please do not misinterpret my emotion of this story, as if I condone the use of weed, because I do not. However, I am realistic to the effects of weed and that weed is legal is some States. So to keep a father away from their child because of his occasional usage is completely ridiculous and absurd to me. Every child deserves to have both parents in their life, especially when both parents are eager to be a part of the child's life. There's nothing more rewarding for a child than to see both their mom and dad at a sporting event, a school play, chaperone a school field trip, or at a friend's birthday party. How is it in the child's best interest to deprive them of these benefits, just because you are mad at their daddy?

The second case I am going to share with you is that of J.A. This one is one for the books, as they say, which is why I added to this book. My client filed a Supplemental Petition to modify his timesharing with his daughter. The parties had a Final Judgment that would allow timesharing with J.A. and his daughter every other week from Thursday after school until Sunday and 2 weeks in the summer and alternating holidays. Their parenting plan, did not provide for additional time during spring break or long weekends. My client resided in 215 miles away from the child and at the time that the parenting plan was established the child was a baby and picking her up on Thursday was not an issue. However, as the years went by the child got older and started school. The timesharing schedule became more complex.

My client would travel the 215 miles, rent a hotel and stay with the child every other Thursday night, so that she can attend school on Friday. After school on Friday, J.A. and his daughter would travel back to his house where she would remain for the remainder of the weekend. My client was willing to continue this schedule, but he felt that since the child is now getting older, he wanted more time with her in the summer and was requesting to have majority of the summer with the child. The mother on the other hand, felt that the schedule was not in the child's best interest. It was too much back and forth. She accused my client of being hostile and aggressive. Not with the child but with her. And because of that she felt that it would be in the child's best interest to have less time with her father. The mother was proposing that the Father have 1 weekend a month, pick up Friday and drop of Sunday, so 48 hours a month, 3 non-consecutive weeks in the summer and alternating holidays.

The issue with these two parents is that there was so much anger between them that they could not agree to anything. There was not one thing that they could see eye to eye on. What school the child was going to attend, what time to call, vacation time, pick up and drop off, extra-curricular activities, absolutely everything was an ordeal.

My client went through 6 attorneys and 5 judges. I judge passed away during the pendency of the case, 2 were rotated, 1 was disqualified and then the final Judge. This case took 3 years have a trial. My client waited for 3 years just so he can request 3 additional weeks in the summer. At the end my client went from having 77 overnights a year to having 90 overnights. No those overnights were not the days he was hoping to get, but overall any additional time with his child was worth it.

The trial was concluded, but do you believe that the fights stopped? Nope. Your right... it did not. Although the Mother wanted ultimate decision making over the child education and medical, the Judge did not grant her that. So this meant that the parties had to continue to discuss major issues that related to the child. So when my client would want to discuss the minor child's school, the Mother would accuse him of making unilateral decisions, being hostile, demanding and manipulative. She did everything in her power to bate my client to lose his cool with her, which wasn't hard since he's feelings for her were none to be desired.

This poor child, has to be exposed to her parent's feelings of resentment for one another. Even if they were successful in not bad mouthing each other in front of the child, their feelings for one another and the mood that they put each other, are surely felt by her.

Should this case have taken 3 years? Absolutely not, any other couple who did not have such hatred for one another would have reach an agreement on the timesharing in less than a year. Having the child spend time with the father on all long weekends, open visitation to the Father with notice at the child's county, every spring break and majority of the summer, is common sense. I spoke about this case with several of my family law colleagues and they all agreed, this case is simple it was ludicrous that they were not able to find common ground in 3 years for the sake of their daughter.

Now if you were to ask each of them individually, they would both tell you the same thing... that they feel like they have conceded in everything and that it's the other person who is making things difficult. And unfortunately for them they are nowhere near the level that they need to be at to be indifferent to one another, which will let them see things clearly.

Again J.A. case is just like J.M, where their ex could not let go of the connection that they had and have allowed themselves to move forward with the emotion of anger and hate. Their decisions are irrational and their actions are driven by anger.

### Healing:

When you finally find peace, or settle for indifference you have reached the point of healing. You do not love your ex, but you do not hate them either, so your actions are clearer and without an ulterior motive.

People who have absolutely no feelings, whether good or bad to another person, do not waste their time going back and forth. If a false accusation is being made, they will either ignore it or response using one or two words, keeping the email very simple and not leaving the door open for a response. They make every effort necessary to avoid long conversations and attempt to keep all emotions out of the little conversations they do have.

The following is a case, from two parents who had moved past their anger and hostility for one another and reached the level of indifference and healing.

I represented the father named J.R. (yes I know I represent a lot of guys whose names start with J..) he and the mother were never married, but they lived together and had two beautiful children. After the parties separated, the mother would not allow J.R. to see his children, everything had to be on her terms. She wanted J.R. to pay for her car, her apartment, the children's private school and give her child support. Well this was not a marriage, so there was no obligation for him to sustain her lifestyle.

He definitely did not have an obligation to buy her a car or pay for her rent. She warned him that if he did not agree, he would not be able to see his kids. The mother was not concerned whether J.R. was a good father or not, because she knew he was, she just knew that his kids were the only thing she could hold for ransom. We attended mediation and were not able to reach an agreement. A few months passed and her feelings for him started to change, she was no longer angry and he was no longer angry at her for using the children as negotiating ponds. They began to talk about the children and together, without me or her attorney, were able to reach a resolution that they felt was in their children's best interest. They settled at a 60/40 split and were able to see eye to eye on the mother's additional request for financial support. Their case settled in less than a year, without the necessity of a Judge to determine their future. They took matters into their own hands and their ability to co-parent should be applauded.

Another case where the parties could amicably resolve all their issues, is that of R.C. My client who was the father, was more stable than the mother. He was able to financially care for the needs of all 3 children and was a great example for them. The mother understood her situation and was realistic that she was not capable of carrying for the needs of all the kids. They set their feelings for one another aside and reached an agreement that allowed my client to have the majority of the timesharing with the children. The mother did not allow her emotions to lead her actions. She knew what was in the best interest of the children and she was thankful that my client was willing to step up and take responsibility for the kids, when she could not.

As you can see, emotions drive our actions either in a positive manner or in a negative one. Unfortunately, most divorce and paternity actions occur when one or both parties are at their highest peak of emotion. The longer that one or both parties holds on to their negative emotions, the longer the case will take. The longer the case takes, the more hostility and defensiveness the parties will feel, which will lead to more negative emotions and the cycle never ends.

We are all adults, and for the most part we hate being told what to do however, the minute that a family law action is filed in the counties I practice, an Administrative Order takes effect and you are to be governed by an order of a judge who has never meet you or your family. They are telling you how to temporarily run your life, until you either figure it out amongst yourself or until another judge who also does not know you, gets to make another decision on how you will now live your life permanently.

The best advice I can give you is to be conscious of your emotions, understand that you may be feeling guilt, fear or anger and that may distort your decision making. Walk away from the situation temporarily and look back at it with a clear mind before you make any life changing decisions that will impact you and your children. It is also very important to manage the situation in a way where the children do not feel responsible for the break-up. Understand that things don't happen TO you, they happen FOR you. Our children are entrusted to us... We were chosen to protect them, to teach them, and to give them an ultimate life. Constant fighting with their other parent will not accomplish those goals.

If you want to learn more about how to have a successful divorce and understanding what you may be feeling during the process, contact our office at **407-704-8932** for a free 30 minute consultation.

# JAMIE C. MANNING, ESQ.

## Manning Law Company,
## Christian Divorce Attorneys

**Email:** jmanning@christiandivorce.us

**Website:** http://www.christiandivorce.us

**LinkedIn:** www.linkedin.com/in/ohdivorceanswer

**Facebook:** www.facebook.com/OHDivorceAnswer

**Twitter:** https://twitter.com/OHDivorceAnswer

**Call:** 614.597.1330

Jamie Manning is an author, speaker, and attorney. She is passionate about removing the stigma from divorce that causes good people to stay in bad marriages for the wrong reasons. As a married, once divorced, adult child of divorce, Jamie's insights into marriage and divorce are unparalleled. Jamie aims to improve the lives of children of divorce by using humour and wisdom to reduce the damage caused by family conflict.

Jamie earned her Juris Doctorate from Case Western Reserve University in 2001 and her Bachelor's Degree from the University of Rochester in 1998. She began practicing family law as a law student and has exclusively practiced family law since 2014.

A professed Christian since kindergarten, her goal is to help you avoid the pain and devastation of an ill-advised divorce or remaining in a damaging marriage. As the owner of the Manning Law Company, she helps clients clearly identify what God is calling them to do to protect themselves, their children, and their finances. Most importantly she stands for the proposition that God loves you and desires for you to have a healthy, fulfilling, and God-honouring life, so you don't have to settle for less.

# YOU CAN FOLLOW THE LORD EVEN THROUGH DIVORCE

by Jamie Manning

*Describe your ideal type of client and the types of situations they find themselves in when they come to you for your help?*

Our ideal clients are good Christians whose kindness is killing them. They have been nice for a very long time believing it was the right thing to do and are now realizing that God must have better for them than this. We stand up for those clients who haven't been standing up for themselves so that they are not bullied and taken advantage of during a divorce. We help these clients gain the confidence they need to rebuild after divorce.

The Manning Law Company's preferred client is an intelligent Christian who is fighting for a worthy cause. Often, our best clients have reached the point where trial is the only option. They have become disgruntled or frustrated with previous counsel whether paid, relative or self and are seeking counsel whose mission and values are aligned with their own. They are seeking an advocate. These are usually child custody cases. Child custody cases are similar regardless of whether the parents need a divorce, have never been married, or is a grandparent seeking custody. They all require the specialized practice of the Manning Law Company. Once we are on the case things move at a much faster rate and clients are able to see an end to the fight.

We also love to work with couples that agree. Some issues of divorce and custody can be resolved using the Manning Law Company's Couple Strategy Session as a springboard to a full and final resolution of matters in dispute. These clients are able to reduce stress, time, and legal fees by settling all matters in the office and never having to appear at court.

*What 3 common obstacles prevent the people you help from achieving their desired outcome?*

## 1. Allowing feelings about the other parent to affect parenting.

Your child's happiness should be the driving force behind your decisions. When I was a little girl my parents divorced and my father had me usually on the weekend. Speaking of times when she picked me up from visits with my dad, my grandmother says: "When I would get you Jamie, you'd be so happy. You'd be sticky and stinky, but happy. When I asked you what you ate you would say. 'Hot peppers and cheese'. But you were so happy." She often tells this story and it resonates with me because the focus was my happiness. Her response could have been so much different. She could have said to me "look at you. He is not washing, watching, or feeding you. You are not going back over there anymore."

They, being my mom and grandma, could have refused to allow me to visit my dad until he became to the kind of parent that they thought he should be. But they didn't. My mom could have been so mad at my father that she used me to punish him by not letting me go to his house. It would have hurt him because of how much he wanted to see me. I am so thankful that she didn't. My relationship with my father continues to be very important to me so hurting him would have hurt me.

Don't let your feelings about the other parent affect your parenting. I know it's easier said than done, but with help and support and good guidance you'll always be able to put your child first. Parents who find themselves unable to control their feelings about the other parent very often unnecessarily increase their own stress, lengthen the time of court litigation, and harm their children. They raise the cost of divorce and custody in many ways that aren't just financial. Most parents' desired goal is to protect their children. The best way to protect your child is to make sure that their happiness is more important than anything that you are feeling.

## 2. Thinking about divorce when you should either be working on your marriage or moving out.

Another problem is thinking about divorce when you should either be working on your marriage, i.e. that is not thinking about divorce, or moving out which is actually beginning a divorce. Usually when people are thinking about divorce they're not actually thinking they're either fantasizing or "fatal"-izing. In any event they're not really thinking. What do I mean when I say fantasizing? I know you think "I'm not fantasizing about divorce," well let me tell you, if when you compare the idea of your life after the divorce to your current life and it makes you smile, you are fantasizing. Or, if you start to think that being divorced is going to be the answer to all of your problems, that's a fantasy. Likewise, if you think that when you're divorced you won't have problems with money, with a messy house, or a messy spouse, fantasy. If you think that when you're divorced everything is going to be so much better -then you are in fact fantasizing. The reality is that divorce is just exchanging one set of problems for another. It is not the answer to all your problems.

On the other hand there are those of you who are completely like I would never fantasize about divorce. Chances are you're "fatal"-izing. In this case when you imagine what life will be after you divorce compared to what your life is like now you think: "Oh my God, I'm going to lose everything. I'm going to lose the house. I'm going to lose the kids. I'm going to lose money. I'm going to lose status. I'm just going to lose and everything is going to be terrible." If this is you, you are "fatal"-izing because while it is true that divorce is just exchanging one set of problems for another, it doesn't mean it will be the end of the world. In fact you may prefer the new problems to the old problems. You have the right to have a healthy, fulfilled life because that's what God wants for you.

You don't have to settle for less than your best life because you are afraid of divorce. Don't avoid divorce because of things that you fear. In this way thinking, divorce is a huge obstacle to reaching a place where you actually have a healthy, fulfilled life rather than an opportunity. Don't be afraid. Many people are harmed by thinking of divorce only in terms of loss without also considering what might be gained. If you know that you have done all you can, that this marriage cannot be saved, and there is no chance of reconciliation, do yourself a favor, don't hold off the inevitable -make a plan and move out. Moving out is not the same as getting a divorce. I am not suggesting that anyone simply quit thinking about divorce, run off, and file divorce papers. Do not leave with that message. That is not the message I'm giving you.

The point is that divorce means I don't want to live with you anymore. I don't want to answer to you when I come and go. I don't want to see you in the morning when I wake up. I don't want to share my life with you anymore. Since that's what divorce means the first step is establishing a separate household, because that's what must happen if you get a divorce. Thinking about divorce is an obstacle that stops some couples from saving a marriage that can be saved and it stops other couple from ending a marriage that needs to be ended.

### 3. Failing to realize that their prayers are more important than words and words are very powerful.

The universe gives us what we want. The universe makes the determination about what we want based on the words that we say. I'm going to say that again because it's important. I want to make sure that you really are listening to this premise so that you can understand the obstacle that we are trying to get you to avoid. The universe gives us what we want and it determines what we want based on the words that we say. What happens very often is the words coming out of our mouths are actually not what we want. If you want a healthy happy marriage you should not be saying, "I don't want to divorce". The universe doesn't hear *I don't want to* all it hears is divorce. If you don't want a divorce, don't use the word. If you say it enough times it will manifest itself. The same is true for saying that you want a healthy happy marriage. If that's what you want then that's what you should say. If what you want is peace you should say that, don't say I don't want to fight anymore because the universe doesn't hear *I don't want to*, all it hears is fight.

Words are very powerful but our prayers are even more powerful. You can't push away something that you're focused on, everybody knows that. It's like the old trick, don't think about the pink elephant, really don't think about the pink elephant. Everybody knows that when you hear that the only thing you're thinking about is the pink elephant. The same is true with our prayers, if we pray so much about the problem we'll just keep manifesting problems. If we pray about victory, if we pray about God getting the victory for us, through us, and on our behalf then victory is what we will see.

You can pray a curse upon yourself by focusing on the problem instead of focusing on the goodness of God. Please understand many of us have been taught a certain way to pray, a certain way to look at God, a certain way even to interpret the Bible. Many of us have been taught particular ways or nuances of our denomination of our family and we mistake those little idiosyncrasies for true faith and spirituality in a relationship with our heavenly father. As a result too many of us end up in the marriages that are not what God would have us to be in while lacking the tools to make them better or the courage to walk away. The words that we speak out of our mouths and in our prayers have a real impact on our lives and our marriage.

*How have you been able to help your clients to avoid or overcome those obstacles and successfully gain the confidence they need to rebuild after divorce?*

One of my favorite clients was divorcing a man who had a good job, but who wasn't good with his money. They had two little girls together. Dad got the girls on Fridays and they would spend the night with him. He didn't get the girls on Friday and Saturday night just one night a week but he did get them one night a week on Friday picking them up from school and then mom would pick them up on Saturday. It never failed she said that sometime on Friday night or Saturday morning the girls would call mom and say, "we're hungry and daddy is too." When I tell this story to crowds full of women you can hear an audible gasp. Right then I have to remind them that dad did get the girls from school on Friday. He didn't just leave them there and not show up.

Mom didn't have to pick her children up from Children Services on Friday because the father didn't come to school like he said he was going to. And he does it every Friday. I explained this to her and advised her that the right thing to do was to order a pizza for them or drop off some sandwiches. See, the rule of thumb is if somebody has to be a jerk let it be the other parent not you. You don't want to be the jerk and in this situation who was going to be the jerk, the poor hungry dad or the mean mother who had the means to feed them and refused? You guessed it, mom would be seen as the jerk in this scenario. The real key is to send the girls with some food on Fridays, if it's a box of cereal and a couple of cans of Spaghettios. It's been a few years since the divorce was finalized and the report from mom says that the relationship between her and dad is getting better. This is a real victory especially for anyone who's gone through divorce. If you're able to maintain some kind of a friendship after your divorce, your divorce was a success. In this case mom's respect for dad and her helping dad to keep him in a good light with the kids helped their co-parenting relationship and this positive co-parenting relationship set the stage for a positive relationship between the parents. This is the gift that the Manning Law Company likes to give its clients. This is the outcome you can achieve when you put the happiness of the child ahead of your own feelings.

Another of our favorite clients was a woman who had been estranged from her husband for some ten or fifteen years. She was an active member of the church, ran a ministry and spread love amongst the congregation. Her children with the husband were adults and they didn't have anything together. In fact I don't think she even knew where he was, but she had never divorced him over all these years because she was taught that divorce was wrong. She was taught that God hates divorce. She felt that getting a divorce was to let God down. It was to turn her back on the marriage vows that she made. Over time she did begin to sense that God was letting her know that she could get a divorce but she wasn't able to afford one. In a rare case we handled the case pro bono and she was granted a divorce. Just months after the divorce was finalized she began dating and she fell fast in love with another member of the congregation. You could see the happiness and the joy all through her. She explained to me how she didn't think she would ever experience love the way that she was experiencing it. I know it was a result of the divorce.

While she was married and still entangled in that marriage vow she wasn't able to open herself up to receive the kind of love that God really wanted her to have. God did not want his child abandoned. God was not going to force her to stay in a marriage that wasn't a marriage and or punish her for being abandoned. That would be jerky and God is not a jerk. Staying in a bad marriage or a dead marriage is not what God wants for anyone. She would have missed the love of her live if had she continued to spend her time thinking about divorce instead of acting on it.

**What are some of the common misconceptions that Christians may have about divorce?**

### 1. God hates divorce.

God hates divorce we've all heard it this. This portion of Malachi which is so often quoted is really just a part of a verse and every verse in the Bible needs to be read in context of the entire chapter and the book as a whole. Let's look at Malachi 2:16 in a number of different translations.

"The man who hates and divorces his wife," says the LORD, the God of Israel, "does violence to the one he should protect," says the LORD Almighty. So be on your guard, and do not be unfaithful. (NIV)

"For I hate divorce!" says the LORD, the God of Israel. "To divorce your wife is to overwhelm her with cruelty," says the LORD of Heaven's Armies. "So guard your heart; do not be unfaithful to your wife." (NLT)

"For the man who does not love his wife but divorces her, says the LORD, the God of Israel, covers his garment with violence, says the LORD of hosts. So guard yourselves in your spirit, and do not be faithless." (ESV)

"For I hate divorce," says the LORD, the God of Israel, "and him who covers his garment with wrong," says the LORD of hosts. "So take heed to your spirit, that you do not deal treacherously." (NASB)

For the LORD, the God of Israel, saith that he hateth putting away: for one covereth violence with his garment, saith the LORD of hosts: therefore take heed to your spirit, that ye deal not treacherously. (KJV)

One thing is clear God doesn't want to see his children hurt and that is why he has disdain for the cruelty these men were inflicting upon their wives by being unfaithful with foreign women and then divorcing their wives. It is important to note that there is nothing in the verse to suggest that divorce is unforgivable or that participating in it disqualifies you from future happiness whether you are the man or the woman. That would be jerky and God is not a jerk.

## 2. Divorce attorneys can't help with custody.

A custody battle is just a divorce without a marriage. A lot of people fail to realize that if you're going down to court with your child's other parent fighting over custody and visitation and child support even if you never got married you're going through a divorce. It's just a divorce without a marriage. In a marriage in addition to the children being an asset that needs to be divided there are often other assets such as the house, bank accounts, retirement accounts, etc. If you and your child's other parent were married and you didn't have any assets and all you had were children together, you'd be in court in the same way. Sometimes people are confused when they hear Christian Divorce Attorney and think we can't help them resolve custody issues. We can help, we have helped many clients in this way.

### 3. Christian Divorce means settling.

Some people when they hear the term Christian Divorce think oh well you guys must do everything very nicely and all your clients want to settle and nobody wants to fight. That is a big misconception. What Christian divorce means is maintaining your integrity throughout the divorce process. It means fighting for the things that are worth fighting for and not fighting over things that aren't worth it. It is a decision to put the children first and to maintain a relationship with God and a clear conscious throughout the process to pave a way for a future that is more in line with what God would have for you. Christian divorce is a new beginning. We understand that as a Christian going through divorce you have given it a lot of thought. We know that you are not moving rashly but that you've given it a lot of consideration. We now trust that you have prayed until God has released you from the marriage and that is a blessing. Nonetheless divorce is still a legal process that involves two people who are angry with one another or worse because that's what divorce does. Christian divorce means putting the good of the whole family before your own personal agenda, even when you don't feel like it.

*What mistakes should Christian people considering divorce be aware of?*

## 1. Hiring an attorney whose values don't align with your own.

Divorce attorneys get a bad name, and many of them for good reason. Sometimes a client's case would have settled but for the attorney they hired. When you're looking for an attorney you want to make sure to choose someone whose advice you can trust. If you feel the urge to go and get a second and a third opinion every time your lawyer tells you something, chances are you have hired the wrong lawyer. You want an attorney who you know puts your goals and your needs above padding his or her pocket. Hiring an attorney whose values don't align with your own may prove to be very costly. It is better to have chemistry and rapport with your family law attorney than to choose a family friend or the cheapest one you find.

## 2. Trying to settle when a settlement isn't possible.

Another problem that we see from many of our clients that are coming to us after they have ended a relationship with their first lawyer is that they feel like they spent a lot of money and a lot of time and that the case hasn't moved anywhere. The case is no closer to a resolution than it was before they started the case, before they spent the money, before they hired that attorney. What we find is that in order to best serve our clients we are aggressive from the outset. You can always start aggressive and decide to loosen up become nice and settle. It's much harder to invest time and energy and money into settlement negotiations and then get aggressive when no settlement can be reached.

### 3. Moving too fast.

As a rule of thumb we suggest that you be separated from your spouse for 6 months. That is physically living at different addresses for six months before filing for a divorce. Sometimes it can't be a whole six months maybe only 90 days, some people can go longer. The key is get the distance from your spouse so that you can do some emotional healing before beginning litigation. You can get a baseline for how things actually work without input from another party. It gives you an opportunity to see what organically happens with the children and finances before you begin spending money to have an attorney speak for you and making court appearances. Sometimes people who have been fantasizing about divorce want to file for the divorce immediately, as soon as the other spouse moves. They think that if they file a divorce fast somehow it's not going to hurt that bad like when you pull a band-aid off quickly, I guess.

The reality is you have no idea how you're going to feel when you get divorced until you get divorced. Divorce is the death of a marriage. It is the death of a dream. It is the death of the future that you planned together. You became one when you got married and there is no way to make one into two without cutting, tearing, or doing something painful.

Mourning has to happen. Different people begin the mourning process at different times. Very often the person who makes the decision to make the move has been making their plan to exit for a long time, sometimes for as long as two or three years and they began the mourning process when they made the decision to not invest any more energy into the marriage. You on the other hand may have been blindsided and will not begin the mourning process until after the spouse moves out. There are a few scenarios when filing for divorce immediately is the right thing to do, those situations are different and you need legal advice to know if you are in one of those situations.

***What common fears prevent your clients from even attempting to achieve their desired outcomes?***

Most people think that lawyers are expensive, even the cheap ones. Frequently, potential clients wanted to work with us but chose a less expensive alternative. What they learned was that this usually ends badly. Often the client feels that the lawyer is unresponsive or not advocating for them in court. By then it's too late. They come to realize the hidden expense of a cheap lawyer. Clients end up with poorly written parenting plans or they end up paying too much or receiving too little child support, all because they wanted to save money on the lawyer.

Another common scenario for clients choosing the less expensive attorney is returning to us because the first lawyer asked for a smaller sum upfront, used it up, asked for more money and then stopped working. We collect a substantial retainer in advance so that we are able to provide a superior level of service without constantly asking the clients for more money.

Dealing with a difficult other parent is stressful and when you have a young child the idea of interacting with this jerk for the next 10 to 15 years is more than you can bear, so you decide not to invest the time and energy into a lengthy custody fight. The reality is, is that what's best for the child isn't always the most convenient for the parent. Some fights are inevitable. Our advice is don't delay. Act now.

The other option is to let the other parent or your feelings about the other parent interfere with your relationship with your child and this hurts the child. Yes, going to court may make things worse before they get better. However, with proper counsel you can invest the time energy and resources into your child while he or she is young. The child will reap the benefits for the rest of their lives. Delay and they may feel the bad effects for the rest of their lives.

Other clients are more worried about the loss in status or reputation. Many of us have heard the story of the couple who just couldn't afford to get the divorce. They realize that if they would separate and stop living in the same house they'd have to begin supporting two lifestyles on the same amount of money that they used to spend on one. Clearly things are going to have to change for somebody at least, if not both of them. It is this loss this change in status that often keeps a lot of people in marriages for too long. This is especially true for persons who are involved in an abusive relationship. Too often they consider losing their material comfort to be a worse loss than losing their dignity staying in the abusive marriage. It's always important to remember and to never forget that God loves you and wants you to have a healthy happy marriage. He wants you to have a safe and a stable life. He wants you to know that He is your provider and that He will take care of you and your spouse.

***It sounds obvious, but why would the people you serve want to achieve their desired outcome?***

Prolonged litigation is not fun. No one wants to be in divorce court or family court for years and years. Many people have had their fill of the process after merely 3 or 4 months. To them it feels like a lifetime but it is a relatively short time to be in court. Nonetheless getting to a resolution sooner rather than later allows the parties to begin the healing process that much faster. It allows them to redirect the energy and resources financial and emotional away from the divorce away from court litigation and back onto things that matter. We think it is very important to never allow clients to be petty causing them to be in court longer than they need to, pay more fees than they need to and experience more stress than they need to. We always help direct our clients to maintain their integrity to make decisions to fight only for the things that really matter and to be willing to compromise and let go of the things that don't. It is this attitude, advice and leadership that helps them to not only reach a resolution that they're satisfied with but at a much faster pace.

People only come to family court because they have to. In an ideal world you would be able to work out all of your family problems without the need for court intervention, unfortunately that just is not reality for many people. If you find yourself in a place where you must go to court, you want an attorney who's going to fight for you, someone who's going to advocate for your position, someone's who's going to understand you and really get behind your case.

We are very selective and only take cases that we can put ourselves behind 100%. We don't take every case because we want to give each of our clients the personalized attention they deserve. We are aggressive advocates who do not waste time trying to settle when a settlement is not possible. At the same time we do not expend your funds trying to go to trial over an issue that can be resolved. It is always our goal to reduce stress, time, and fees. For some of our clients the goal has nothing to do with stress, time or money. It has only to do with the best interests of the child and making sure that their child remains in a safe and stable environment.

The rare couple that is able to end their marriage or decide custody of their children amicably have higher rates of never returning to court, better relationships and healthier children. The effects of high-conflict divorce have been found to be harmful to children. Sometimes they can't be avoided, but if they can it is the next best thing to avoiding court altogether.

### What led and inspired you to get involved in this field?

As an adult child of divorce, I never thought that I would be divorced. I was intent on doing all that I could to maintain a marriage that would last a lifetime. I was confident that it would work out after all I had done everything right. I read the Power of a Praying Wife, always tried to please him and not nag. Instead I took all of my gripes to the Lord. I was very active in my church and kept a regular daily devotional time. But I still ended up divorced. I prayed constantly for my marriage and my husband and still I ended up divorced. A marriage takes two committed people and my husband had checked out when he decided not to heed the promptings of the Holy Spirit.

I can pinpoint when the end of the marriage began. I recall a conversation we had shortly after I had been praying intently for him to change his attitude about a number of financial issues. He said to me that he should change his mind in all of the areas that I had been praying about. I was thrilled that my prayers had been answered. I realize now that he said he should not that he had changed his mind. It was a message to me that God was knocking on his heart and that he chose to ignore him.

I had been an attorney by profession for years before I lived through my own divorce. It was that experience that made me an authority on the subject. I recognized the need for someone to help Christians like myself whose marriage ended even when they didn't want them to. All of the literature I found condemned me when I know that I serve a loving God. Christian Divorce Attorneys was born to stand against the proposition that divorce is an unforgivable sin and that you are doomed to a loveless life and disqualified for service in the Kingdom because you participated in a failed marriage.

**What are your final thoughts for Christian people considering divorce?**

Divorce is not a road that you want to travel unadvisedly. Just like marriage requires planning, prayer, and counsel, so does divorce. Each person has to answer to God for him or herself whether or not they are divorcing for right or wrong reasons. Regardless if you did the right or the wrong thing in getting married or divorced, know that God still loves you. Even if your family, friends, and church turn on you, God still loves you. Seek wise counsel from non-judgmental Christians and legal counsel from a Christian Divorce Attorney.

**If the reader wants to know more, how can they connect with you?**

You are worth the time and effort it takes find the right lawyer. Christians throughout the state of Ohio who want to maintain their integrity while going through the divorce and custody process can reach us by phone at **614.597.1330** to schedule an appointment or sign-up for our newsletter at www.christiandivorce.us.

# ROBERT J. SALZER, ESQUIRE, LL.M.

Family Law Attorney

Williams Family Law, P.C.

**Email:** RSalzer@BucksFamilyLawyers.com

**Website:** www.BucksFamilyLawyers.com

**LinkedIn:** www.linkedin.com/in/Bob-Salzer

**Call:** (215) 340-2207

Robert J. Salzer, a Partner at Williams Family Law, P.C. in the Philadelphia suburb of Doylestown, Pennsylvania, focuses his practice on a variety of family law matters, including alimony/spousal support, divorce, equitable distribution, marital agreements, child support, child custody and prenuptial and postnuptial agreements.

Prior to joining Williams Family Law, Mr. Salzer served as Deputy District Attorney for the Bucks County District Attorney's Office where he handled legal matters related to toxicology, vehicular homicide and appeals. Previously, he served as a law clerk for the Honorable Robert J. Mellon of the Bucks County Court of Common Pleas.

An experienced trial attorney, Mr. Salzer has conducted presentations across the Commonwealth of Pennsylvania regarding techniques to improve cross examination, particularly as it relates to expert witnesses.

After earning a Bachelor of Arts in English Writing from the University of Pittsburgh, Mr. Salzer went on to earn a Juris Doctor from The Catholic University Columbus School of Law. In 2016, he earned his LL.M in Taxation from Boston University School of Law.

# WHAT CLIENTS NEED TO KNOW BEFORE FILING FOR DIVORCE

By Robert J. Salzer

**Describe your ideal type of client and the types of situations they find themselves in when they come to you for your help?**

My ideal client is a man or woman who is initiating or has been sued in divorce and/or custody and whose marital estate is of moderate to substantial wealth. When coming to me, clients are trying to determine what rights they have and how they can best preserve assets or be distributed assets they mistakenly believe belong to the other spouse by virtue of title.

**What common obstacles prevent your clients from achieving their desired outcome?**

I am frequently asked about obstacles to reaching a successful outcome. The most common obstacle I see occurs when a client initiates a case with unrealistic expectations of its ultimate outcome. While there are occasionally instances where prospective clients are pleasantly surprised by what I tell them to expect from the distribution of the marital estate, more often than not, clients feel either that they should be distributed more or that their spouse isn't entitled to as much as I believe the law and facts dictate. It is common for the "wronged" spouse to feel that he or she should be entitled to a greater share of the marital estate because of cheating, lying, abuse or a litany of other behaviors. In reality, the legal system doesn't bog itself down by analyzing who did what to whom during the marriage and then inflicting punitive sanctions on bad spouses. That fact can, unfortunately, be a bitter pill to swallow for an aggrieved spouse.

A second common obstacle is dealing with the reluctance of some of my clients to be sufficiently aggressive in pursuing a recommended course of action. While aggressive tactics aren't always necessary, failing to use them as needed can have tremendously negative effects by giving an opposing party a psychological, if not tactical, advantage. Convincing passive and naturally non-aggressive clients to follow my lead can be challenging and requires a shift in the mindset of a client that doesn't necessarily occur overnight.

A third common obstacle is one beyond the control of my clients, but something that will directly impact their cases, that being the selection of legal counsel by opposing parties. It is a misconception that it is advantageous when opposing counsel is "bad," as incompetencies will create more problems and exhaust more resources than would two seasoned professionals. If a case isn't resolvable, two experienced and pragmatic attorneys will cut right to the heart of the dispute and agree that the unresolvable issue (or issues) must be litigated. A less experienced or qualified attorney will cause everyone to get bogged down in nonsense that, although often resolved by the courts favorably to my clients, exhausts resources and time that could otherwise have been used to focus on legitimate disputes in the case.

**How have you helped people who are initiating or have been sued in divorce and, or custody?**

In my profession, we don't use the word "fair" since the law, the facts of divorce and life are frequently unfair. That said, when it comes to developing appropriate expectations, there are few things more important for a client than immediately getting advice from a qualified expert in the field of matrimonial law who can, based upon experience, take the cursory facts of an individual case and advise the client of what the end goal should be.

It's hard to appropriately strategize if we don't know what the ultimate goal is and how to best reach that goal. Similarly, we must both be working towards the same goal or an appropriate relationship between counsel and client cannot exist. While correcting unreasonable expectation and setting appropriate ones isn't always easy, it's a crucially important part of the job.

As part of my initial consultations, on many occasions, potential clients have told me upon hearing my initial advice that another attorney advised him or her that the outcome would be dramatically different and more favorable than I expect it to be. My response is always that "you should hire that attorney. I only ask that when things don't go your way, you remember this conversation." Family law is the division of assets and parents' time with the children; to do it right, a good attorney frequently has to tell clients things they might not want to hear, but need to hear. I always give me clients' honesty, and expect the same in return.

An important factor in any divorce action is actually beyond a practitioner's control: who was retained to represent the spouse? I frequently say to clients that there are four (if not more in higher net-asset cases) persons involved in each case; two lawyer and two litigants. If any of those four are unreasonable or irrational, the entire case can be screwed up. While I can't control my adversaries, it is best to know their strengths and weaknesses and know how to play them to my clients' advantages whenever possible. I am first and foremost a firm believer in having a "home court" advantage, meaning hire someone who practices primarily in the area in which a given matter will be litigated. Knowing the members of the local family bar and having experiences against them teaches me their strengths and their weaknesses. I believe in cases where opposing counsel is making a tactical error that it is best to never interrupt one's adversary when he is making a mistake and that there are times where giving your adversary enough rope to hang himself is the best tactic.

Recently, in a matter where the parties are dividing in excess of $100 million, the best move I could make was the one I didn't make and the plan worked perfectly. Dividing assets is a game of chess; when your adversary is playing checkers, recognize it and stay the course.

Commonly, for a variety of reasons, my clients are so used to acquiescing to their spouses that they have lost the ability to stand up for themselves. While one might stereotypically think that it's the wife who can't stand up to her husband, in actuality, it is frequently the reverse. Divorce is gender neutral or possibly same-sex. Regardless of the circumstances, I frequently am my client's voice and, when needed, backbone.

I frequently tell clients there are few things I enjoy more than wrestling control away from a control freak. It is of crucial importance to be aggressive, but appropriately so. Some practitioners, presumably masking for their own insecurities, are incessantly aggressive. The problem with that approach is that one can only play hard ball when in possession of the ball. When bargaining from a position of strength with clients who are used to folding their tents rather than confront their spouses, there are no better times to aggressively advocate and empower the clients to realize, with a little prodding, they are stronger than they realized.

**What are some of the common myths about divorce that your clients believe to be true?**

Divorces are fraught with myths and misconceptions. The most common of client misconceptions is that all of the marital assets are going to be divided equally when, in the Commonwealth of Pennsylvania, equal division of property is rarely the case. It is common for one spouse to receive a disproportionately larger percentage of the marital estate based on a variety of factors that must be carefully weighed and analyzed. There are instances where I have advised clients who are privately negotiating with their spouses as to what I think should be considered a "win," which sometimes allows them to successfully broker the terms of agreements I then draft and that distribute to my clients assets in excess of what could have been expected in litigation.

Similarly, clients frequently believe that keeping assets separate or separately titled insulates them from division as part of the divorce proceedings when, generally, title is wholly irrelevant. New clients commonly and proudly tell me that they have kept their incomes in accounts titled solely in their names and are devastated to learn that incomes and assets acquired during marriage are subject to distribution regardless of title, but for a few exceptions, the most notable of which is the receipt of an inheritance. When analyzing assets that were brought into a marriage, it is important to understand how to best isolate from the marital estate as much of the assets' value as possible since any increase in value during coverture of pre-marital assets is subject to distribution.

A common misconception among small business owners, as many of my clients are, is the belief that the existence of the business at issue before marriage removes it entirely from the marital estate. In Pennsylvania, the appropriate analysis is far more complicated, and sophisticated knowledge of business valuations, appraisals and impact of the tax effect of a hypothetical liquidation can ultimately make differences of tens, if not hundreds of thousands of dollars. Marital estates involving business interests, perhaps more than any other cases, require the careful analysis of a qualified profession to understand the nuances of business valuations and how they apply in instances of divorce.

*What common but unknown pitfalls should someone considering their options for divorce be mindful of?*

Common pitfalls, which I tend to recognize when I am retained midway through a case where my new client has dismissed another attorney, exhibit that laypersons, who are otherwise extremely well educated and intelligent, can be sold a bill of goods by a less-than-qualified attorney.

First, hire someone whose primary area of practice is family law. While there are many excellent general practitioners out there, would you rather have the local mechanic work on your Ferrari or a certified Ferrari mechanic who works primarily on Ferraris? Given the potential expense to properly navigate a divorce, the analogy is apropos.

Along those lines, the adage "you get what you pay for" is true across all areas, including legal representation. It's tempting to hire someone whose rate is low or whose retainer is small, but know that the market sets the prices. You should never bargain shop for things like Lasik surgery and lawyers; there is simply too much at stake.

That said, beware of lawyers whose retainers are non-refundable. Within the last year, a client who was dissatisfied with her prior counsel and retained my services early on in her divorce, brought me her file to review. I knew from what I was seeing that no more than a few thousand dollars worth of work had been performed at that point and, knowing what my client's former legal counsel required as a retainer, I advised my client to request the balance of her old retainer be returned.

After attempting to do so and being told the retainer was non-refundable, my client brought her ex-attorney's fee agreement to me for review. Sure enough, in black and white, it stated all retainers were "non-refundable." It was a tough and unfortunate lesson for my client, a bright and well educated woman, to learn about reading everything you sign.

The lesson is to read a fee agreement and ask questions if you have them. I won't accept a dime from any clients who have not fully read and understood my fee agreement, which includes a provision that any unexhausted portions of their retainers are refunded upon request. You shouldn't be paying anyone for work that was not performed. In the event you aren't required to sign a fee agreement when retaining an attorney, that should set off alarm bells. You are entering a contractual relationship with your attorney; the terms of that relationship should be committed to writing.

*When faced with the realities of divorce, what are your clients most fearful of?*

The most common distress for a client is created by a fear of the unknown. Many of my clients have been married for greater than 20 years and can barely recall what life "alone" was like. Everyone experiencing a divorce needs a support network, which includes legal counsel. I am not a therapist for my clients, but frequently tell clients I am their navigation system as they drive into the unknown. Ignoring the navigation system is likely to cause one to end up alone and lost, but it is important for a client to know he or she is in the driver's seat as I guide with advice and experience. Therefore, the greater fear may sometimes be whether or not you are.

First and foremost, there must be a comfort level on the part of the client, which naturally leads to a trust between attorney and client. When that exists, the third most common fear, that of losing, whatever a "loss" in a given case is perceived to be, should dissipate. Legal counsel is there to think logically, so you don't want an attorney emotionally invested in a matter as emotions cloud judgment. I care about my clients and their cases tremendously, but I have no emotional investment when I step into a courtroom or a settlement conference.

**It sounds obvious, but why would your clients want to achieve this outcome?**

Winning in family law isn't like most other areas; there isn't a big payday or punitive damages imposed, nor is there a conviction that validates a claim of wrongdoing. Family law involves the division of assets and time, such that it isn't always clear what should or shouldn't be considered a "win."

To win in the division of assets means to exhaust all available remedies permitted by law to retain or obtain, depending on the viewpoint, not only as many assets as possible, but also the best assets available to ensure long-term accumulation of wealth and security.

*What led you to this field?*

While there are a number of attorneys in my family, I can't say their influence affected my career choices. I can say that, once I realized playing center field for the Yankees was not in the cards, I knew being an attorney was what I wanted to do. I've always been adversarial when feeling wronged and enjoy standing up for myself, so taking those skills and entering a profession that is adversarial by nature and that allows me to stick up for other's rights was a natural fit.

My degree in English Writing taught the necessary skills to effectively write as an advocate while law school sharpened my skills to apply reason and logic to given fact patterns and to adjust on-the-fly whenever an unexpected moment occurs, especially in court. When training young prosecutors, I always told them that, especially in front of a jury, no matter what happens or is testified to, make sure to act like you knew it was coming. Perception is reality.

*What are your final thoughts for someone who is considering divorce?*

There are three specific skill sets a client in need of a family law attorney should look for. First, while ideally a case never requires actual litigation, given that most cases end up in a courtroom at some point, did you hire a litigator? For me, litigation is the most enjoyable part of the job. Having spent nearly seven years prosecuting thousands of cases, with my focus on trying vehicular homicide crimes, courtrooms are as comfortable to me as my own office. I have been able to take the desire to help victims of crimes to my family law practice, where helping clients through difficult and emotional periods of their lives is very rewarding.

Second, especially when trusts or business interests are involved, did you hire someone with an understanding of complex finances and tax ramifications? Within a few years of beginning my family law practice, I realized this was an area I wanted to strengthen and, despite a personal pledge to never again take a test after the bar exam, I enrolled in school yet again to obtain a legal master's degree in federal income taxation, which I was awarded in 2016. While difficult, that education has been invaluable when it comes to litigating higher wealth and more complex cases.

Third, did you hire someone who can write well? It's a common misconception that all attorneys are well written, and the complaints, petitions and motions drafted by your attorney may be the first thing a judge or arbitrator sees about your case, so the form in which they are drafted and the content of such documents are crucially important. As an English writing major in college whose law journal note was published in law school, my first legal job as a judicial law clerk assisting in writing legal opinions came naturally. As a prosecutor, I frequently wrote by own legal briefs for convictions that were appealed to higher courts and took that same concept of writing as an advocate into my family law practice. Find an attorney who knows the courtroom, the complexities and how to commit your arguments to written word and the odds are that you'll be in good hands.

If the reader wants to know more, how can they connect with you?

Anyone looking to retain the services of my firm must first pass a check to confirm there are no internal conflicts, which is performed by one of my legal assistants. Once the conflict check is clear, a consultation can be set up, normally within days of the first contact. Please visit my firm's website at www.bucksfamilylawyers.com or call my office at (215) 340-2207 for further information.

# HOWARD PERITZ, ATTORNEY

## The Law Offices of Howard Peritz

**Email:** howard@howardperitzlaw.com

**Website:** www.howardperitzlaw.com

**Call:** 847 562 5880

Howard Peritz is an attorney with experience as a sole proprietor, managing attorney and a senior associate in Chicago and the surrounding suburbs, providing legal services in family law and bankruptcy. Currently, Howard is a sole practitioner with his office in Deerfield, Illinois.

This enables him to provide his clients with legal representation in Cook, Lake and McHenry Counties, Illinois. For more than 30 years, Howard has demonstrated himself very effective in litigation, negotiation and mediation and has a keen vision for developing and executing successful action plans.

His work consistently results in favorable decisions and settlements that greatly benefit his clients. Howard is a proven project manager, team builder and mentor who becomes a valuable advocate of each project or case he undertakes. Howard is also an active networker and connector who understands the value of bringing people together.

# CALCULATING CHILD SUPPORT

## By Howard Peritz

Spousal maintenance also known as alimony calculations differ from state to state. Not to be politically incorrect but in most cases, the Husband is the payor so for purposes of this chapter, I will use Husband as the payor and Wife as the payee. In Illinois, my home state, the legislature created a calculation to determine maintenance as of January 1, 2016. Prior to a change in the law that went into effect January 1, 2016, the issue of maintenance was almost exclusively at the discretion of the trial judge. This led to seriously inconsistent results from judge to judge.

From my personal experience, I can tell you that prior to the change in the law, in a single case where the settlement conference was held before one judge but the trial was before a different judge the case went from being a no maintenance case during the settlement conference to having maintenance awarded at 10% of the Husband's net after child support following the trial.

Commencing January 1, 2016, first the determination has to be made that the situation warrants maintenance. In cases where both parties earn substantial amounts of money, even if the Husband's income is substantially more than the wife's, it may not be a maintenance case. Or, if the wife has substantial non-marital assets, the Court may determine that maintenance is not warranted.

Once the determination is made that maintenance is warranted, the calculation is made. To calculate the Husband's maintenance obligation, take thirty percent of the Husband's gross income and subtract twenty percent of the wife's gross income. The result is the husband's maintenance obligation to the wife with one exception. In no event may the wife's income (including maintenance but excluding child support) exceed forty percent of the joint gross income of the parties.

Then, there is a determination of the duration for which maintenance is to be paid. Illinois has determined that for marriages less than five years from the date of marriage to the date of filing the divorce proceedings, the duration of maintenance is twenty percent of the duration of the marriage. For marriages of at least five years but less than ten years, the duration of maintenance is forty percent of the duration of the marriage. For marriages of at least ten years but less than fifteen years, the duration of maintenance is sixty percent of the duration of the marriage. For marriages of at least fifteen years but less than twenty years, the duration of maintenance is eighty percent of the duration of the marriage. For marriages of twenty years or more the

Court has the discretion to award either permanent maintenance or for a duration equal to the duration of the marriage.

This method is only used, however, for parties whose joint income does not exceed two hundred fifty thousand dollars.

Moving on to the issue of child support, many states, including Illinois prior to July 1, 2017, moved to what has been called an income share method of determining child support as opposed to the percentage method. Again, not to be politically incorrect, as the Husband is usually the payor and so I will use him as the payor when discussing child support. Under the percentage model, the state determines a percentage of the Husband's net income based upon the number of children the parties share. In Illinois, those percentages were:

| Number of Children | % of Husband's Net Income |
| --- | --- |
| One Child | 20% of Net Income |
| Two Children | 28% of Net Income |
| Three Children | 32% of Net Income |
| Four Children | 40% of Net Income |
| Five Children | 45% of Net Income |
| Six or More Children | 55% of Net Income |

Depending on the situation, this model can be terribly unfair to the Husband. Where Husband's and Wife's incomes are seriously dissimilar the percentage model may not be unfair. Where both Husband and Wife make similar, significant incomes, the percentage model can be unfair to the husband.

Under the income shares model, the government makes a determination, based upon the parties' joint income and the number of children they share, of the cost of raising children. Then Husband pays a percentage of that amount. Many of the states that have moved to the income shares model use federal guidelines to determine the cost of raising children. Illinois has chosen to have the State determine its own guidelines.

While these guidelines are statutory, they are not absolute. Judges have the authority to impute income to either the Husband or Wife. If the Wife has a degree but is not using it to generate income, the Judge can impute income to her. If the Husband is unemployed or underemployed, the Judge can impute additional income to him. Judges also have the authority to deviate from the guidelines either upward or downward. In those situations, however the Judge must make specific findings as to the reasons for the deviations.

Now, let's look at some examples of each of these examples.

Seth and Sarah Perry got married on May 20, 2005 and live in Buffalo Grove, Illinois. They have two children, Elizabeth, born on March 12, 2007 and Quint, born on August 11, 2010. Seth is in sales and earns one hundred twenty thousand dollars annually. After Elizabeth and Quint started school, Sarah went back to school and became a teacher and earns sixty thousand dollars annually. It is now July, 2017 and the magic that was once there between Seth and Sarah is now gone from their marriage.

Sarah goes to see a Matthew Kraus, a well-known divorce lawyer and wants to know what she is entitled to from Seth on a regular, monthly basis. Matt explains to Sarah that there are two separate issues here, alimony or what is now frequently referred to as spousal maintenance or support, and child support. Matt explains that spousal maintenance differs from state to state but, in Illinois, as of January 1, 2016, the state legislature gave divorce lawyers specific guidelines for maintenance. Before 2016 it had been at the complete discretion of the judge. Now, there is a specific formula to determine maintenance. Matt goes on to explain that the first hurdle is a determination of whether Sarah is actually entitled to maintenance. This issue is at the discretion of the judge but Matt tells her that she is more than likely than not to receive maintenance because of the significant difference in Seth's and Sarah's incomes.

The next determination is, how much maintenance Sarah will receive. Matt explains that under the new law, the formula is thirty percent of the payor's (Seth's) gross income minus twenty percent of the payee's (Sarah's) gross income. In Sarah's case, the calculation will look like this:

|  | Seth | Sarah |
|---|---|---|
| Monthly Gross Income | $ 10,000 | $ 5,000 |
| Percentage to apply | 30 | 20 |
|  | $ 3,000 - | $ 1,000 = $2,000 |

Sarah would receive two thousand dollars per month in alimony or spousal maintenance except for one provision of the statue. In no event will the party receiving maintenance receive more than forty percent of the parties' combined gross income. In Sarah's case, forty percent of their joint income is six thousand dollars. If Sarah were to receive two thousand dollars in maintenance, she would be receiving seven thousand dollars per month or 46.67 percent of the parties' joint income. In Sarah's case, she would only receive one thousand dollars per month in alimony or spousal maintenance.

Matthew then tells Sarah that, based upon the twelve-year two-month marriage, she is entitled to maintenance for a period of time equal to sixty percent of the duration of their marriage. Sixty percent of a one hundred forty-six-month marriage calculates to eighty-eight months or seven years four months of maintenance.

Next, Matthew explains child support. For years, child support was based upon certain guidelines percentages applied to the net income of the payor, usually, the Husband. Net income was defined as income, from all sources, minus taxes, health insurance premiums and employer mandated deductions. In Illinois, the guidelines percentages were:

| Number of Children | % of Payor's Net Income |
| --- | --- |
| One child: | 20% of Net Income |
| Two children: | 28% of Net Income |
| Three children: | 32% of Net Income |
| Four children: | 40% of Net Income |
| Five children: | 45% of Net Income |
| Six or more: | 50% of Net Income |

Based upon these percentages, under the percentage model, let's see what Sarah would receive. For purposes of this example, we're going to assume that Seth pays three hundred dollars per month for health insurance (yes, I know health insurance is usually significantly higher but Seth has a very generous employer). The calculation would look like this:

| | |
|---|---|
| Seth's Monthly Gross | $10,000.00 |
| Maintenance Obligation | 2,693.00 |
| Income tax based upon a filing status of single | |
| With 1 exemption | 300.00 |
| Health Insurance | $ 6,007.00 |
| Net Income | $ 6,007.00 |
| 28% for two children | x 0.28 |
| Seth's child support obligation | $ 1,682.00 |

As a result, Sarah will receive Two Thousand Six Hundred Eighty-Two Dollars per month for maintenance and child support. One Thousand (the spousal maintenance amount) will be included in Sarah's income for purposes of income taxes and deductible to Seth, and One thousand six hundred eighty-two dollars per month would be tax neutral to the parties. After allowing for taxes, Seth's and Sarah's monthly incomes after maintenance, taxes, child support and health insurance will look like this:

|  | **Seth** | **Sarah** |
| --- | --- | --- |
| Monthly Gross | $10,000.00 | $ 5,000.00 |
| Maintenance | $ (1,000.00) | $ (1,000.00) |
| Income tax | ($ 2,693.00) | $ 997.00 |
| Health Insurance | $ (300.00) | |
| Child support | $ (1,682.00) | $ (1,682.00) |
| Net income | $ 4,325.00 | $ 6,885.00 |

Sarah winds up with Sixty One percent of the joint net income. Understand that, under this method of calculation, Seth's child support obligation does not change whether Sarah works or does not work at all or if she makes One Hundred Twenty Thousand Dollars per year. I know that the people responsible for paying support are saying this is unfair while the people receiving support think it is eminently fair.

Now let's look at the income shares model. Thirty-Eight States have now moved to the income shares method of calculating child support which takes into account several factors including the Payor's gross income, the Payee's gross income and the cost, according to government tables, of raising children based upon the joint income of the parties. Many states use federal guidelines to determine the cost of raising children. In Illinois, (the Perry's home state) however, the Department of Human Services has developed its own guidelines. Now the picture is quite different as you can see below.

| | Seth | Sarah Joint |
|---|---|---|
| Gross income | $10,000 | $ 5,000.00 |
| Maintenance | $(1,000) | $ 1,000 |
| Taxes | $ 3,011 | $ 997 |
| Net Income | $ 6,999 | $ 3,579 |
| Joint Net Income | | $10,578 |
| Percent of income: | 66.17 | 33.83 |

The Illinois Department of Human Services has determined that, based upon a joint net income of Ten Thousand Five Hundred Seventy-Eight Dollars per month, the cost of raising two children is Two Thousand Two Hundred Two Dollars per month. Applying the percentages to that amount and Seth is responsible for One Thousand Two Hundred Fifty-Six Dollars per month for child support.

Percentage of Combined Net Income

66.17                    33.83

Illinois' Determination of Cost of Raising Two children

$ 1,457.06              $744.94

Total: $ 2,202

Under income shares, Seth's child support obligation is reduced because this model recognizes both parties' obligation to support their children. It also recognizes the lifestyle the child would have enjoyed in the absence of the divorce.

Now, let's look at an example where the parties' incomes are closer together. Under this example, let's assume Sarah's income is One Hundred Thousand Dollars. There will be no maintenance at this point because Sarah's income is already forty-five percent of the parties' joint income.

|  | **Seth** | **Sarah** |
|---|---|---|
| Gross income | $10,000 | $ 8,333 |
| Taxes | $ 3,011 | $2,024 |
| Net Income | $ 6,999 | $ 6,308 |
| Joint Net Income | $13,297 | |
| Percentage of Combined Net income: | 54.54 | 45.46 |

Under the income shares method, the cost of raising children grows as the parties' joint net income grows. Illinois has determined that for parties whose joint net income is Thirteen Thousand Two Hundred Ninety-Seven Dollars the cost of raising two children is Two Thousand Four Hundred Forty Dollars. Applying the percentage of combined net income the result is:

Illinois' Determination of Cost of Raising Two Children

| Seth | Sarah | Total |
|------|-------|-------|
| $ 1,330.78 | $ 1,109.22 | $ 2,440.00 |

In Illinois, things change depending upon the number of overnights each parent has. If the parent who is paying child support, in our case, Seth, has at least one hundred forty-eight overnights per year based upon the parenting plan, the calculation changes. In such case, the guideline amount to raise a child is multiplied by one and one half and the percentages are reversed. The reasoning is that Seth will have additional expenses as a result of having so many overnight visits with the children. He might need a larger home; he will definitely need more food; he may need to have clothes at his home. In our example with Seth earning one hundred twenty thousand per year and Sarah earning sixty thousand dollars per year the math changes as follows:

| | |
|---|---|
| Cost of raising two children | $2,202.00 |
| Seth has 148 over-nights or more | 1.5 |
| | $3,303.00 |
| Reversal of percentage | 33.83 |
| Seth's obligation | $1,117.40 |

Seth's obligation is reduced by $213.38 to assist him in the additional expenses he will incur by virtue of the increase in child rearing expenses for him.

While the above seems fairly simple and easy to calculate, any couple contemplating divorce where there are no children, no marital property and no significant non-marital property should consult an attorney and not attempt to perform these calculations on their own. Many different things can happen.

I am currently litigating a case where the husband has non-marital assets in excess of $1,000,000, an annual salary of $120,000 while working for his father, and approximately $500,000 in marital property. Wife has been caring for the two children for the twelve years of the marriage. In a settlement conference, the Judge "recommended" that the Husband give wife all of the non-marital property in addition to giving her $7,500 per month net in child support and maintenance. $7,500 net is equal to approximately $9,000 gross which means Husband would be paying wife $108,000 of the $120,000 salary. How can the Judge justify such a deviation from the guidelines? He has imputed additional income to the Husband because he works for his father.

In the final analysis, you need to have an attorney who is experienced in the law and is familiar with the Judges before whom he or she appears. To schedule a free initial consultation, call us at 847-562-5880.

# DOUGLAS KATZ, MBA, CDLP

## Vice-President, The Federal Savings Bank

**Email:** dkatz@thefederalsavingsbank.com

**Website:** www.divorcelendingpro.com

**LinkedIn:** www.linkedin.com/in/douglaskatz

**Facebook:** www.facebook.com/DougKatzVPMortgageBanker

**Call:** 708.829.1336

Doug Katz graduated from the United States Military Academy at West Point with a Bachelor's Degree in Behavioral Science and Leadership Management. After graduating, he served five years in the US Army as a Field Artillery Officer. Following his military service, Doug spent several years in the telecommunications industry working in the operations and marketing for a major equipment manufacturer in the Chicago suburbs. During this time, he also earned his MBA from Loyola University Chicago.

Doug moved to the mortgage industry based on a desire to help people realize their dream of homeownership and to accomplish their real estate investment goals. Throughout his career, he has consistently used his expansive knowledge, practical experience, work ethic, and exceptional customer service to help his clients achieve their goals. Doug leverages his skills and talents to solve problems quickly and efficiently through the mortgage process. While he has experience serving all types of clients, Doug specializes in divorce lending and has a strong understanding of the unique challenges they face.

# NEW HOME, NEW START - PLANNING FOR A MORTGAGE DURING YOUR DIVORCE

By Douglas Katz

*Who is your ideal client, who do you help?*

If I were to ask you to list the five most important priorities associated with a divorce, I am confident that your home would be listed near the top. This, after all, is where you sleep, eat, raise your kids, et al. This is not surprising as over 80% of married couples own their own homes. In short, the vast majority of divorces involve the sale or refinance of at least one residence. The disposition of the residence is always addressed in the divorce decree, but this only reflects the required final disposition and the details of getting to that end state are left unresolved until the end. This is where the problems begin.

Since getting a mortgage loan involves borrowing money in one of the most highly regulated industries around, the devil is in the details. It is the HOW of dispositioning the existing home or acquiring a new home that is rarely addressed. This is where I, as a qualified and certified divorce lending professional, I am essential. While a mortgage generalist can get simple loan transactions across the finish line, they are often ill-equipped to deal with the challenges associated with a separation or divorce. In short, a subject matter expert is required.

Additionally, divorce lending is as much about a high-touch consultative process as it is about the transaction. For many lenders, volume is key and they do not have time to spend working closely with the client and their team of professionals. This should, however, be a requirement as you decide on a lender. I, for example, do my best to be at the table with the client's attorney and financial advisor to provide input and expertise as to how a particular decision will impact a real estate transaction. I am available to them to provide guidance and feedback on how to best enable my clients to purchase or refinance a home.

My job, however, is not limited to the nuts and bolts of structuring a deal or helping craft the real estate components of a divorce decree. Supporting my clients transcends dealing with specific nuances of family law and IRS tax laws as they relate to real estate in divorce situations. These are, without a doubt, important and necessary, but there is an emotional component that cannot be disregarded. Many times, I am a coach, a cheerleader and sometimes even informal therapist. Because of this, I always take the time remember that this a time of great stress and turmoil, which requires the right touch.

So, in a nutshell, my clients are a relatively simple segment of the population. They are normal everyday people who just want to own their own home but who find themselves in the very complex and difficult situation of a marital dissolution. They are people who need help planning for and navigating the complex and sometimes confusing world of mortgages. They are people who need a coach, partner, advocate and subject matter expert. They are people who need me and it is my passion to be there for them to help them realize their aspirations and to help them begin the next chapter of their life with the security of owning a home.

**What common obstacles prevent the people you work with from getting a loan during a divorce?**

Contrary to what most people think, it is not necessarily anything specifically related the mortgage itself that is the main obstacle to buying a home during or subsequent to a divorce. Rather it is an ignorance as to how a mortgage works that creates the largest obstacle. This ignorance leads to bad planning and a disconnect between the mortgage and all of the other components of a divorce. As a result, the decree often reflects solutions that do not sync up with lender guidelines and requirements. This can often be a significant enough dissonance that the loan is denied for insufficient income, insufficient assets or some other lender guideline. Additionally, this lack of awareness drives them to make bad decisions and they do not hire a divorce lending specialist to reduce and hopefully eliminate this blind spot.

Since banks want to get paid back, serving the debt is a cornerstone of the loan approval. Because of this, banks and other institutions that write home loans have specific detailed guidelines which they use to assess and calculate a borrower's income. This where the second major obstacle generally emerges. When a household is split, the income is as well. Meanwhile, the cost to live for each of the spouses during the separation and through the divorce typically goes up. Income is diluted as a result and qualification becomes much more difficult.

This is compounded for the spouse who will be receiving maintenance and child support as this is an income stream which had not been verified for a long enough period of time with enough consistency to be used for income calculations. Even if the borrower can secure employment or better their employment, there are requirements for employment and income history that can negate using the income. This is especially prevalent with variable income types such as commission overtime and bonus, where a history is required to utilize the income for debt service calculations. While there are some fantastic niche programs that improve a borrower's ability to overcome income issues, maximizing income and getting a client's debt ratio within tolerance is often the biggest challenge.

Finally, I see credit hits as the third most common obstacle to getting a loan during a divorce. As I have repeatedly said, separation and divorce are an emotionally charged time where people are not generally themselves. They sometimes use things like paying bills and debt as a means to strike at one another by not servicing the debt as required by the lender. Credit card, car notes and even mortgages go unpaid sending BOTH individuals credit scores into a tailspin. It does not take long for stellar credit to become average or even poor. Since credit score and history are key components of loan approval, this can complicate or even eliminate the ability to get a loan. Lending institutions will not factor in who was supposed to do what, even if it was by court order. So my advice here would most definitely be to avoid this often self-inflicted obstacle.

*How have you helped past clients to avoid or overcome obstacles and successfully finance a property around a divorce?*

All mortgages have a similar set process that is generally followed from application to funding, but a specialized lender can use different programs in concert to create a solution to complex issues created by a divorce. To effectively problem solve, a good lender will let go of the traditional mortgage paradigm when creating a solution for a client. This is a critical reason to use a specialized, divorce focused lender when buying or refinancing.

I recently had a client who reached out to me during the resolution phase of her divorce. The process was dragging on much longer than expected and she wanted to buy a home. In this case, she had already vacated the marital home and was renting. She had spoken to some other lenders with less experience in this field, who had given her bad information on obtaining a loan. One, for example, communicated to her that she needed a full two year history of receiving maintenance payments to verify her income, which she did not have.

By the time she came to me, she was pretty despondent. She had been generally told that she would not be able to buy a home. As part of my process, I dig deep to fully understand the client's situation and, by doing so, I was able to get the right information. I found discovered that if the divorce were completed, she would have substantial assets and maintenance, but was currently receiving set payout per a separation agreement. Discussions with her lawyer revealed that she could petition for some of the assets that would be awarded her later for this purpose.

There are very few, if any, programs in the marketplace that will allow fit this unique situation. There are, however, some non-traditional programs that will allow the use of assets to create income. Working with her attorney, we structured a two-step approach under which I would do a short-term loan for using her assets that I would later refinance into a more traditional loan after the decree was finalized and her financial situation was clearer and more definite.

*On a day to day basis, what common misconceptions do you hear from clients wanting to finance a property around a divorce?*

I have heard numerous times in my career, "it's just a mortgage, how hard can it be to get done?" While this can sometimes be a fairly accurate statement under the best of circumstances, any potential borrower needs to understand that they are borrowing money in one of the most highly regulated and stringent industries around. Everything about a mortgage is scrutinized to ensure that the process is fair and equitable for all applicants, which leaves little room for gray or subjective decision making. Since many situations involving divorce or separation are fraught with complex and complicated challenges, to assume that the divorce mortgage lending process will be easy or that it will be similar to a previous process can and is a calamitous assumption.

The aforementioned challenges are further complicated when borrowers confuse the legal aspects of their agreements or divorce decrees with the requirements to get a loan approved. I hear more times than I would like to share comments like my divorce decree says that he or she needs to do pay the mortgage on the existing home, pay particular credit accounts, pay me support, et al. This may well be true from a legal perspective, but for a lender these must be documented. An ex-spouse not paying a mortgage or other requirement as directed by a decree, thereby, damaging a borrower's credit will not be overlooked. Failure to pay support on time or in full contrary to a divorce decree is in breach of the decree, but a lender will not use the full required amount in the decree unless it can be verified.

Finally, many borrowers fall into the same paradigm of commoditizing the lender and institution. They believe that all lenders are the same and that they can all perform as required to get the deal done. In reality, however, a specialist like a Certified Divorce Lending Professional is infinitely more qualified to anticipate and deal with the complexities of a divorce mortgage than a generalist. In the week before authorizing this chapter, I had no less than three clients come to me with serious misinformation as to everything from how long they need have documented spousal support to count as income to how to manage a refinance where one ex-spouse was buying out another. This volume of questions is constant and it is the fortunate ones who find a specialist like me BEFORE the go down a path of higher cost on a loan or catastrophe when they are erroneously required to sell the home or worse short sell it.

### *What unknown pitfalls should the people you help be aware of?*

Benjamin Disraeli once said, "To be conscious that you are ignorant is a great step to knowledge." I really love this quote because it hits at the heart of where things go wrong when buying or refinancing a home during or after a divorce. That is not to say that people are stupid, but rather that they lack the knowledge required to make the right decisions, which can lead to bad decisions.

The first thing that I see time and time again are borrowers who choose the wrong lender. For whatever reason, they do not choose a lender like me who specializes in divorce related lending. This like going to a general practitioner when you need a knee rebuilt. Now I am not saying that the generalist is not a good lender. I know and work with many who are fabulous. My point is that there are so many unique components of divorce lending that you need someone who can anticipate the challenges and work actively to minimize or negate them. This entails coordinating with the other members of your team to integrate the mortgage into the total divorce resolution.

Picking the right lender only works if you empower them to help. A key component of this is timing. It is better to avoid the snake than to treat the bite and bringing the lender in early provides a better path toward ownership. I have personally seen many clients not get me involved early enough. This shifts the process from a proactive approach to a reactive approach, where it is much harder to achieve positive results.

Finally, I see emotion get in the way of logic and pragmatism. I want to be careful here to not minimize the emotionally charged nature of a divorce or separation. While I have seen amicable divorces, this, in my experience, has been the minority. More often than not, the split is less than cordial at best and street fight at its worst. Financial matters become a preferred weapon where bills or support go unpaid damaging credit and complicating efforts to document future income. I have learned through my Aikido training that to hurt someone else is to hurt one's self and this cannot be more true here. Usually, both spouses end up losing and undermining their own situation in the process.

***What common fears prevent your clients from financing a property around a divorce?***

I have found that clients working to finance a property around a divorce have different fears based on where they are in the process. Initially, prior to even filing, the fear is that they will be discovered by a friend, family member or even their spouse. They are usually not ready for this information to become public. This is a completely legitimate fear with something like a mortgage where credit will be pulled and some documents require the signature of both owners, however, this can definitely be managed. The beginning discussions should be consultative in nature with a focus on advice and planning. I myself always provide the highest confidence and discretion to my clients regarding their personal information and defer to them as to what should be shared with any other party.

Secondly, I see a general fear of the unknown regarding the home. When they signed on the dotted line and bought the house, most people generally thought that they would be leaving on their own terms. It does not matter if it was 20 days or 20 years prior, the home was something that they could depend on. Now they have no idea as to whether or not they can afford to stay and, if not, what they will be able to afford in a new home. This can sometimes paralyze them into not seeking assistance at the appropriate time. This can often be because they think that the divorce decree will eliminate this uncertainty, but as far as loans are concerned it cannot.

Finally, I see a post-divorce fear of rejection. I hear again and again from my clients the same basic introduction, "You probably cannot help me, but..."For whatever reason or through experience, they have been denied with previous efforts at resolving their home financing needs. They feel that it is a fool's folly to begin the process again. As I further inquire as to their situation, I see that a plan for resolution did not accompany their earlier denials and, without a plan, resolution and success is far less likely. This is again why it is so hugely important to pick a lender who is completely invested in the success of their clients.

*It sounds obvious, but why would the individuals and or organizations you serve want to finance a property around a divorce?*

Michel de Montaigne once said, "My home...it is my retreat and resting place..." I sincerely think most people would concur with his sentiment. After all, homeownership is a core component of the American dream which permeates our collective psyche. Aside from that, homeownership fulfills a primal need for stability and security. It grounds us and provides a safe place for the homeowner.

During a divorce the need for security is amplified as the individuals embroiled in the split have their lives turned upside down and every which way. It is during this time more than ever that the home takes on a meaning synonymous with security. Anything that provides a stable footing represents a base for which to move on to the next phase of their life.

If there are children involved this need for stability is amplified. Aside from the same need for security and safety as their parents, the children often have roots in their community in the form of schools, sports and other extracurricular activities. Their friends, which for them provide the moral and spiritual support, are also likely heavily tied to the community. The home is their connection to their lives, so proper resolution insulates them from the tumult of the divorce. Even if the home is new, it can provide the stability that they needs. I recently did a deal for a client who could not afford the marital home, but was able to buy a slightly more modest property in an adjacent community that shared a school system. Solving this one issue made all the difference to her young children.

Beyond the security and stability, the home is a huge component of one's identity. In some cases, the home was where scores of memories were formed. Events like kid's birthdays, dinner parties, and holidays all took place in the walls of the house. The connection to who they were in those times can be what gets someone through the tough time as they struggle to assess and deal with an uncertain future. In other cases, a new home represents a physical manifestation of a new identity. It is a clean slate from which new explore new opportunities and independence.

There is a purely logical side to this as well. The home is typically the largest marital asset. The disposition of it is essential for both parties to move on. Whether it is selling it outright or buying someone out, the home needs to be divided. Often times, this requires a refinance to pull out equity as well as to pay off the existing lien. This requires a new mortgage and although not a new purchase is definitely a realization of the homeownership goal.

This is why if you are considering a divorce and need to finance a home, it is so essential pick wisely and to choose the appropriate lender to meet your needs. Peace of mind regarding the home can provide you safe harbor in at least one aspect of your life, but only if you are well represented. Oddly enough, I can compare it best to hiring someone to do the electrical work on your home.

You can choose and handyman or an experienced electrician. Both can get the job done, but when you lay your head on your pillow every night, which one will give you confidence that nothing will short or even worse catch fire. My guess is the specialist, the electrician. This decision is no different and when you lay your head down every night during the divorce, the fears about your home should not be what keeps you up.

*What led you to this field?*

I get asked a lot about why I decided to build my practice in such a difficult space. After all, the deals are difficult and the stories can be heart breaking. While there a lot of happy endings, there are also times that I cannot help a client, which is tough. From a practical perspective, I spend a good amount of time on activities that will not result in me earning a dime. You would think I would be crazy to pursue building a business this way. There is one thing that working with this group does afford me and that is the fulfillment and self-actualization that comes from really helping people in one of the toughest times of their life and for me if I am not helping people, I mean truly helping people, there is no reason to work.

For me the journey to this point was a deliberate one guided by the principles of Aikido and major life event of my own. The Aikido came first and, as I trained and rose through the ranks, it provided me a spiritual awakening and a purpose. The art promotes harmony, peace and leaving the world a better place than you found it, which I began to embrace and apply to my work. Prior to that I was a good loan officer and a manager, but, like many in my field, it had become a job. I was changing in my perspective and practice, but then it happened.

I was sitting in a recovery room in the ICU of the cardiac unit at Loyola University Medical Center recovering from an aortic replacement surgery. To provide context, I born with a congenital heart issue that often results in aortic aneurysms and I had developed one that had reached a critical point requiring intervention. So lying in a bed with medical equipment stuck to and stuck in my body, I realized my mortality and that there is precious little time to make a difference as my spirit now wanted to do.

I recovered quickly, more quickly than most in fact. I was training again within 90 days and went on to earn my Sho Dan or black built less than a year after my surgery. This made it 100% apparent to me that like fighting back physically, I needed to actively find and pursue the opportunity to help people. Reality and pragmatism made it clear to me that many options were just not practical, I was a lender with almost two decades of experience and that was where I needed to bring this effort.

As I inventoried my career for the times that I truly made a difference, divorce came to the forefront. The times where I was able to provide positive support and assistance to a client during their divorce and separation. The sincere gratitude that they felt and communicated to me enabling them to have a new start or to secure a home to care for their children just kept re-emerging. I myself came from a divorced household, so this was something that I understood. It was then that I decided to devote the core of my business to divorce mortgage lending.

In the time since, I have worked to bring my experience and resources to this effort. It is my aspiration to shift the role of the lender from the transactional to the consultative for my divorcing client. It is my goal to move the role of the lender from the technician to the specialist who actively collaborates with the rest of the divorce team and influences the process to best enable my clients to get a new start and realize the dream of homeownership.

**What are your final thoughts for the reader who is wanting to begin the next chapter of their life with the security of owning a home?**

With all that I have said prior, I want to end by highlighting that the mortgage process is simple but not easy. You apply, you send in your documents, your loan gets approved or declined and you either close or move on. This simplicity, however, can be catalyst for failure as prospective borrowers commoditize the lenders confusing simplicity with ease. Even when a borrower understanding that their situation is unique and different, they fail to make the connection between lender capabilities and the potential problems with their deal. This can and does lead them to making the wrong choice.

This is really not the borrowers fault. The internet and media have convinced them that mortgages are about speed and price and that service and expertise are secondary. To get a loan done fast and potentially never speak to your loan officer has some become an aspiration goal. When confronted with the colossal challenges that accompany a divorce mortgage, borrowers fall prey to slick marketing and rate myopia, but hey fail to see that low cost is inconsequential if the loan does not close. This is why I was so happy to co-author this book.

You have read throughout my chapter about credit issues, income challenges and everything else that makes a divorce mortgage different. You have seen through examples that reactive thinking, lack of planning and bad decisions can negatively impact your ability to finance a home. You have also seen that picking the right lender early in the process and working with them to develop a plan can have amazingly positive results. This is what I would see as a no brainer.

So, my recommendation is actually as simple as the loan process and actually just as easy. If you are considering a divorce or even in the midst of one and if you want to buy or refinance a home, hire a good lender who specializes in divorce lending and empower them to help you. Finding one may be a bit harder or less convenient than going into your bank branch, but the rewards are worth the time. Find out about their experience, credentials and, most of all, character. Ensure that they specialize in divorce lending and that they will take care of you.

***If the reader wants to know more, how can they connect with you?***

I believe in learning about my clients as well as educating them. I offer all of my clients a free, no obligation consultation to discover their needs and to devise a plan. As part of this, I also provide all of my clients a free divorce mortgage kit, so they can learn more about how to finance their home.

I can be reached through any of the following methods:

**Website:** www.divorcelendingpro.com

Call: 708.829.1336

# ABOUT THE AUTHOR

Mark Imperial is a Best Selling Author, Syndicated Business Columnist, Syndicated Radio Host, and internationally recognized Stage, Screen, and Radio Host of numerous business shows spotlighting leading experts, entrepreneurs, and business celebrities.

His passion is discovering noteworthy business owners, professionals, experts, and leaders who do great work, and sharing their stories and secrets to their success with the world on his syndicated radio program titled "Remarkable Radio".

Mark is also the media marketing strategist and voice for some of the world's most famous brands. You can hear his voice over the airwaves weekly on Chicago radio and worldwide on iHeart Radio.

Mark is a Karate black belt, teaches kickboxing, loves Thai food, House Music, and his favorite TV show is infomercials.

Learn more:

www.MarkImperial.com

www.ImperialAction.com

www.RemarkableRadioShow.com